The Splendor of His Music

THE ADVENTURES OF TWO AMERICANS IN POST-SOVIET UKRAINE

DIANE McMURRIN

WINEPRESS WP PUBLISHING

The Splendor of His Music
© 1998 by Diane McMurrin

Printed in the United States of America

Packaged by WinePress Publishing, PO Box 1406, Mukilteo, WA 98275. The views expressed or implied in this work do not necessarily reflect those of WinePress Publishing. Ultimate design, content, and editorial accuracy of this work is the responsibility of the author(s).

ISBN 1-57921-114-3
Library of Congress Catalog Card Number: 98-60491

Surely you will summon nations you know not,
and nations that do not know you will hasten to you,
because of the Lord your God, the Holy One of Israel,
for He has endowed you with splendor.

—Isaiah 55:5

This book is dedicated with love to my mother,

Ellen Hagler Nash Godshall

You gave us all you had to begin this mission. You prayed for us every day, and longed for the day we would return.

Today we can't go back to the way we were, but we will someday be reunited complete in Him.

Until that day, I long to share this story with you.

Contents

Chapter 1

I Don't Know Where I'm Going

W here *is* Ukraine?" I asked my husband as we opened the empty suitcases on our king-size bed. "I know it's near Russia, but I've never seen it on a map." We were standing in the house of my dreams, a spacious home in Winter Park, an exclusive suburb of Orlando, Florida. I had loved this house ever since we moved here three years ago: its hardwood floors and large windows looking over the backyard with its rose gardens and hanging bougainvillea.

"Here! See if you can find it," replied Roger, tossing me a lightweight jacket with a map of the world printed on it. Made of thin, space-technology material, the jacket was a souvenir I had bought at the Space Museum a few months ago. Printed across its back was the continent of Asia.

Roger is a born teacher. He often answers my questions with a suggestion, forcing me to find the answer myself. Thirty-five years ago, he had been my new vocal music teacher in high school when I was the senior choir accompanist. Even then I felt attracted to his enthusiasm for living. He inspired his students to go beyond themselves—to achieve the impossible.

I closed the lid of the suitcase and stretched the jacket across it, searching for Ukraine. "This large green spot south of Russia? So that's where we're going!" I said with a laugh. Tomorrow our trip would take us over ten thousand miles, and we didn't know where we were going!

Roger and I were accustomed to traveling. In the past twenty-five years as director of music and arts in several large Presbyterian churches, Roger had taken choirs of all ages on tours to Europe, the Orient, South America, and Canada, as well as to major cities in the United States. I had assisted him by conducting the children's choirs and, at his encouragement, had taken several tours myself with my girls' choir. Before full-time church work, Roger had been a professor of music at Otterbein College in Ohio where he taught music education, voice, and choral groups. Roger was endowed with a high-energy level, a love of people, and a persistent desire to make his dreams come true. His enthusiasm inspired others around him to believe in "the dream"—whatever his focus was at the moment. Our twenty-eight years of marriage had seen many of these dreams fulfilled through hard work and steps (sometimes leaps) of faith. Though I was less comfortable with risk taking, I would follow him anywhere.

Planning this adventurous trip to Ukraine began a few months earlier when we were having lunch with George McCammon, an Episcopal priest, and his wife, Toni, in Orlando, Florida. We had first met George in 1990 when we were organizing a choir tour to Russia. His Eastern European contacts agreed to assist us, but, after the house arrest of Gorbachev, our choir members were too afraid of the instability of Russia. The tour was canceled.

Now in 1992, George had been living in Kiev, Ukraine, for the past three months, where he had started a church and a humanitarian aid ministry. He told us some of his struggles there. His downtown apartment had been burglarized for the second time. The thieves had taken everything, even his clothes. George had an engaging sense of humor, and when he laughed, he made me feel that even his problems were fun. He was moving to a safer neighborhood across the river where he had rented an apartment for his family, who would join him in a few months.

In her fashionable glasses and chic, short haircut, Toni seemed almost too sophisticated to be a missionary. Besides assisting George in organizing the Church of St. Andrew, which he had begun, Toni, an elementary school teacher, would train teachers and supervise the Sunday school classes for children. She had not always been enthusiastic about moving to Ukraine, but one night she had a dream that left a profound calling on her life. There were crying children who could not be comforted, and God had told her she must answer the cry of the children. When she awoke, she was crying. Since that night, she knew she had to go.

George also shared a vision he had had in Kiev, and a voice said, "It all begins here." He was so certain of it that he had resigned his pastorate in Orlando and was moving his family to Ukraine. Matthew, their sixteen-year-old son, would accompany them and finish his education through home schooling.

We knew nothing of such experiences. Our world was America, and the everyday work at our downtown church involved many choir rehearsals, worship services, concerts, tours, and staff meetings. We told George and Toni that, although our year had been wonderfully exciting, we were really exhausted and were looking forward to our month of quiet vacation.

"Why don't you come to Ukraine?" George offered. "The finest musicians in the world are there. The Ukrainian people love classical music. Perhaps you could give a concert—maybe Handel's *Messiah*. No one has ever performed it there before—at least not during the past seventy years of Communism. It was forbidden."

A crazy idea! Go to Ukraine for our vacation? George and Toni were now offering to find us a place to live and help us advertise the concert. I looked across the table at Roger and saw a dangerous glimmer in his eyes. Even with his salt-and-pepper hair, his countenance seemed younger than his fifty-three years. Making music was the energy that drove him, especially when that music had a spiritual purpose, and even I felt warm to the idea. Ukraine would be an adventure, and I wanted to do something significant like George and Toni—for a brief time at least. I could not fathom a permanent attachment.

"What about the danger of Chernobyl?" I asked. "How far is it from Kiev?"

"It's seventy miles north, but most people say it is safe now. You'll be fine. Just don't drink the water. Bring a distiller." Toni spoke matter-of-factly, as if Chernobyl were the least of her worries.

Before we knew it, we were making definite plans to spend five weeks in this country we knew nothing about. "You'll love it!" George said to Roger. "It's like riding the rapids on a rubber raft. You never know what to expect. You just hold on and pray."

Now three months later, we had gathered our vacation pay and study leave allowance, a $500 donation from a friend plus some personal savings, one hundred pounds of borrowed vocal and orchestra scores, and were packing for our trip to Ukraine. Our fifteen-year-old son, Matthew, would be traveling with us.

Roger decided to bring more music than just Handel's *Messiah*. "We might be able to learn this," he said, as another bundle of music went into the suitcase, which was already overweight. I was more concerned about eating, so my suitcase contained canned tuna, macaroni-and-cheese mix, Slim-Fast drinks, granola bars, and lemonade powder. Matthew took so many summer clothes that we would probably not have to do laundry the entire five weeks. He also took his basketball. His six-foot frame and muscular arms would be helpful in carrying the luggage filled with heavy music.

While at the Miami airport, Matthew saw many things to explore. He is just as adventurous as his father. He was still not back at the departure gate at the last call for boarding. The German airline that we were flying paged him, but they could not pronounce the name "Matthew McMurrin" with any recognizable English sound. Roger ran through the shops, frantically searching for him while I boarded the airplane and prayed. Was this an omen? Finally I saw Matthew coming down the aisle alone. "Where have you been?" I asked, as if it mattered.

"Don't worry, Mom! The plane doesn't take off for five more minutes," he explained casually.

Meanwhile Roger, unaware that Matthew was on board, was ready to leave Matt's passport, ticket, and his American Express card to come on the next flight to Munich. "I think your son is now on the plane," said one of the attendants. Two minutes before takeoff, Roger came breathlessly down the aisle to join us, his black silk shirt soaking wet with perspiration. With an exasperated sense of relief, he sank into his seat and fastened his seatbelt as the plane began to move. We were off!

The next morning we arrived in Munich. From there we traveled by train to Budapest through Vienna. We knew Vienna, we'd heard about Budapest, but beyond that point was the "unknown," just a large green spot on the back of my world jacket.

Until we reached Budapest, it was impossible to buy a train ticket into the country of Ukraine. As the Vienna train arrived slowly under the canopy of clouded glass in the Budapest train station, we felt as if we were entering a World War II movie set. Was this really the year 1992? The station was dingy yellow, gray, and black. Compared to America or Germany, Hungary lacked color, and the people, dressed in black and gray, were not smiling. *This is what a communist country must be like,* I thought. *So little joy!*

We entered the small international ticket office. One attendant sat at the desk. She spoke little English and wrote the tickets by hand. There were no computers, yet they accepted American Express. Fortunately there was space on the train to Kiev that night. We left our luggage in the guarded luggage room and spent the few remaining hours exploring the city. The Parliament building and a church across the river were the only sights we could classify as "attractive." We ate our last hot meal at a nice restaurant, which also served us a pitcher of ice water, and headed back to the station.

At 9:00 P.M. the three of us were on the platform beside an old Soviet train with khaki cars. Lifting the four hundred pounds of luggage onto Wagon #5, we climbed aboard—ticket and bread and sausage and Coca-Cola in hand. Our conductors, two very large Russian women named Olga and Ludmila, showed us the compartment that would be our home for the next twenty-five hours. Roger bought the women each a canned Coke and an ice cream. They were delighted.

The train was extremely warm, and I could feel the sweat trickling down my back. We waited at the open windows in the hall, peering out like prisoners waiting to be taken to a camp of an undisclosed location. At 9:15 P.M., the train began to move. As the lights of Budapest faded, life as we knew it disappeared behind us. Ahead lay an unknown world wrapped in a cloak of darkness.

Chapter 2

No Man's Land

A Soviet train is a strange experience for a Westerner. The compartment has four bunks, two on each side. The lower bunks can be used for sitting during the day, but they are too deep to be comfortable for very long. The bench seat lifts up to store luggage underneath. The window in the compartment is nailed shut because the Soviets wanted to keep people from escaping either into or out of the train. Under the window, attached to the wall, is a small shelf to hold food and drink. There is no dining car on the train, so all food must be provided by the passenger. In summer, flowing air circulates from a vent into the compartment, but one cannot have the fan and electric light operating at the same time. For an extra charge of one dollar, the conductor brings dull, gray sheets (slightly damp) and a square pillow that spits feathers when fluffed. My sheet had a hole in it.

A toilet room is at the end of each car. There is no toilet seat, no toilet paper, and no soap. The train wobbles so much that using the facilities is like riding a bucking bronco. There is a metal handle on the wall directly in front to hold for balance. Otherwise, one would surely be thrown to the dirty floor, which is always wet.

The three of us filled the compartment with our luggage. Fortunately no fourth passenger joined us. Since we knew no Russian except "Yes," "No," "Thank you," and "Goodbye," we were more comfortable not having a Russian-speaking stranger among us. It was stifling hot, and the lazy flow of air from the vent took more than an hour to bring relief. Every time the train stopped, the air flow stopped too, and the temperature began to rise. Then the air flow stopped completely, and the overhead light came on. Roger climbed to the top bunk and opened his favorite book. He likes to read when he travels. Matthew lay on the lower bunk across from me, and the motion of the train soon lulled him to sleep. I closed my eyes and tried to sleep while it was possible, for I knew that tonight would have several interruptions.

At 2:00 A.M. the train came to the Hungarian-Ukrainian border. Three sets of guards boarded to check passports and visas. With each set of guards, the faces were younger and the eyes harder. As the last young man took my passport, he scowled at me, looked at my passport picture, and again gave me an intimidating stare. I was afraid to smile. What would that mean? Would he think I was a spy trying to cover my true identity? Should I try to match his stoic mood? I felt guilty, and I had done nothing wrong. Matt was forced to sit up out of a sound sleep and open his eyes, which he did with much difficulty. Roger lifted his head from the bunk and tried to make cheerful conversation, none of which was acknowledged by the young man. The last guard left us, and we turned out the light.

Roger and Matthew went back to sleep, but I could not. I waited for the train to move again, but it remained still. The lights from outside were shining in my eyes through the window. I sat up, looked out, expecting to see buildings. But there were none, only trees. The spotlights were on top of tall poles far above the trees. The strong lights pierced the darkness for a short distance, ending in a curtain of black. This was no man's land—the area between the borders of Hungary and Ukraine—and the purpose of the bright lights was to prevent illegal crossings.

I moved into the hallway of the car where the windows were opened six inches from the top and looked out, listening to the sound of rain upon the leaves. Its gentle music was incongruous with the oppressive mood of this "no man's land," where men had been shot trying to escape to the West. I stood with my face close to the open space of the window, drinking in the damp night air.

The train jerked forward once again, this time approaching a complex of large cranes. An American student in the next compartment had told me what was to follow: the changing of the wheels.

Each wagon is detached from the train and lifted by a crane ten feet into the air, leaving the wheels on the track. The old wheels are rolled away and new ones are rolled in. The wagons are then lowered, and the new wheels, attached. This is necessary because the tracks in Ukraine (and all other former Soviet countries) are of a different gauge (width) than their Western neighbors. The gauge is a deterrent to foreign invasion by rail. During this process no one is allowed to leave the train, and the toilet rooms are locked. The deafening sound of metal wheels banging into each other makes sleeping impossible. The entire procedure lasts three hours.

It was during the banging of the wheels that Roger became very ill. Evidently, the water he drank at the Budapest restaurant contained bacteria that was now playing havoc with his stomach. With the toilet and the windows locked, he was in an emergency situation. I quickly improvised a solution, pulling some Zip-Lock bags from the suitcase. I hurriedly handed Roger one of the larger bags, and he deposited his supper into it. The banging continued, the compartment was stuffy, and I again returned to the hallway for fresh air.

Finally, we were rolling on our new wheels into the darkness again. We were in Ukraine, and I fell asleep exhausted from the vigil.

Shortly after dawn I woke up, feeling cold. The temperature had changed. I looked out the window to see large mountains. *This looks like the landscape of Switzerland,* I thought. We were in the Carpathian Mountains of western Ukraine. As we came to little towns nestled in the valleys, I realized this wasn't anything like Switzerland. The buildings were shabby, needing paint and repair. The roads were rutted with mud, and weeds were everywhere. Piles of junk lay along the roadside. The people, poorly dressed, walked in the mud, carrying burdens on their backs. The land had been trampled by Communism, promising equality and prosperity but delivering slavery and poverty. No one, however, could destroy the beauty of the mountains, and my eyes traveled upward to see the majesty that only God can create.

After ten hours of train travel, we still had fifteen long hours to go. I rationed the bread and salami, one sandwich at 8:30 A.M. and one more at 3:30 P.M. I ate in the hall because Roger, still sick and motionless in the top bunk, could not stand the smell of food. The train stopped at a small town, and the American students next door got off, returning with newspaper cones of fresh raspberries they had purchased from the old women next to the tracks. They offered me some of their prize, but I refused, even though the berries looked delicious. Were they washed? Washed with what? I took no chances. I didn't want Roger's disease.

We passed through more than a hundred miles of farmland without a single fence. This had been the breadbasket of Europe. The black topsoil is three feet deep. Hitler had hauled this valuable soil by the truckload to Germany during World War II. Stalin had created a famine in the 1930s, stealing the grain from the farmers, forcing them to give their farms to the State, and selling the grain on the international market to build buildings in Moscow. Six to ten million Ukrainians died of starvation. Now the farms all belonged to the government, but they were not productive. Only one-third of the produce got to the marketplace. The rest either rotted in the field unharvested or lay waiting for trucks that never arrived. There was not enough fuel.

The landscape changed by evening. I saw birch-tree forests partially shielding the flickering, red sun. I sat by the window catching the last of the natural light, reading a traveler's pamphlet about Ukraine.

Ukraine had been the birthplace of Christianity for Eastern Europe, before Moscow was even a tiny village. Norsemen from Scandinavia had influenced the ancient culture since the 900s, and Greek monks had brought the first written language called Rus. The Age of Kiev Rus, A.D. 980–1240, was a prosperous time for this rich land. Since then, the country had been invaded by many nations and tribes. Its people knew nothing but servanthood. Except for a few months Ukraine had never been free, until now.

The sky became dark again, the air flow stopped, and the lights came on. Soon we would arrive in Kiev. I packed all the miscellaneous items back into the suitcases, including the Pepto Bismol, the plastic bags, and the address book containing George and Toni McCammon's phone number. I could hardly wait to take a shower. My last one had been fifty-five hours ago, and my clothes were as grimy as I was.

Roger was sitting up now, playing cards with Matt. I was glad to know he was finally feeling better. Our strange and uncomfortable journey was almost over. Ahead lie George and Toni and a sense of normalcy. This is what I thought awaited us. Boy, was I ever wrong!

Chapter 3

Lost in Darkness

The train slowed as it approached the station in Kiev. Then it stopped. "Are we really here?" I asked Roger, peering out the window. "It is so dark."

I looked at my watch—11:15 P.M.

Since Roger was still weak from dysentery, Matthew and I pushed and carried most of the luggage to the end of the car. I got off first, stepping down into almost total blackness. Matthew handed the suitcases to me. We were at the end of a very long train, the car farthest from the station. There were no carts or porters to help us. We saw some shadowy figures approaching in the mist. At any moment we were expecting to hear George's congenial voice calling, "Roger! Diane! Hey, Matt!" But the crowd came and left. George and Toni were not among them, and we were alone. Our hearts sank.

Roger decided to leave Matthew and me with the luggage so that he could search for George and Toni. Matthew sat down on the pile of suitcases. I paced nervously around them. The only other person on the platform was a muscularly built young man who came to us selling souvenir pens and military medals for a dollar. He was very persistent, but I knew that his products were overpriced. One dollar, though not much to an American, was a day's wage for a Ukrainian. Besides, I was not in the mood to buy anything.

Forty minutes later we saw Roger coming back alone, looking very tired. He told us he had found an "Information" booth inside the terminal. He waited in the long line of people for almost fifteen minutes, but the line was not moving. When he went to the front to investigate, he found the attendant sleeping. Miraculously he found his way back to our platform after searching many stairways that led to the tracks below. George and Toni were nowhere to be found.

"What do we do now?" I asked, and nothing came to mind.

"*You* have their telephone number," he complained, shifting the responsibility back to me.

The telephone number was stuffed into one of the large suitcases, but I could not remember which one. I was hesitant to open them because I had seen a gang of youths, one of them clutching a woman's purse, running on the opposite platform.

"I don't think it's wise to unpack all our things right here. It's too dangerous," I said. "Besides, I don't even have enough light to see what I'm searching for."

The darkness started closing in upon us. Here we were—late at night—with no one to meet us. We couldn't speak Russian; we couldn't carry all our luggage; we had no place to go; Roger was sick; and I was wearing $2,000 in cash around my waist. We were helpless, yet something must be done. We couldn't just sit on our suitcases until daylight.

The young man who had tried to sell me souvenirs came back, saying, "Taxi?" We knew we had to get out of the dark, and this boy was our only connection. We conveyed to him, mostly in body language, "Yes, we want a taxi. Will you help us with the luggage?" He took off his belt and connected the two heaviest suitcases. The larger one weighed over seventy pounds. Then he slung them onto his shoulders, picked up two more, and moved toward the terminal at a good clip. The three of us, carrying the five remaining suitcases and two backpacks, followed him. Roger was kind to give me the smaller bags, and I took the lead, chasing after this stranger.

As we climbed three sections of steps, we intermittently held our breath against the putrid smell of urine from the bottom of the stairwell. The smudged glass doors at the top swung open to reveal a long waiting room stretching across the many tracks below. We passed through hundreds of people slumping in chairs or lying on the dirty cement floor. It was a painting in gray I shall always remember: gray room, gray light, gray people—shabby, hopeless, lonely, and poor. I felt suspended in a dark cloud, but then reality hit me, and I saw the medal salesman quickly moving across the room. We had to catch him. Looking back, I saw that Roger and Matthew had stopped for a moment to rest their overloaded arms. Afraid we would lose our leader, I pressed on through the crowd with a sense of desperation.

I followed the salesman into another passageway which led to the top of a large T-shaped staircase overlooking the main terminal below. The stairs descended down, down, down into another mass of people, swirling across the floor like muddy, agitated water. The medal salesman was halfway down the steps at the T-crossing. I turned and with relief caught a glimpse of Matt's head twenty yards behind me. Hopefully Roger was with him.

My feet clicked a fast rhythm down the steps as I wove my way through the people climbing up the steps from the level below. A large statue of Lenin loomed above me at the center of the staircase, as if he were surveying his creation. "This is all your fault!" I muttered to him, wanting to shake my fist in the air.

The young man with our baggage was quickening his pace through the crowd. Memorizing his position, I descended to the floor level and zigzagged through the crowd. When Matt and Roger got to the main floor, I lost sight of them.

"Mo-men-tey!" I yelled at the speeding bullet ahead of me, hoping to find a word that would communicate. At the time, I didn't know that the word was Russian, but it sounded foreign, and he did respond by slowing down, at least temporarily. I used the word again and again. My fear pulled me in two directions. I was afraid that the stranger would steal our suitcases of precious music, and I wondered if I would forever lose Roger and Matthew, swallowed up in the faceless crowd. I rolled my eyes upward to see a massive iron chandelier with dim electric candles adding to the mood of gloom and doom. We were nearing the end of the room, and the medal salesman was heading toward the right exit door. I was five seconds behind him.

Outside the station I was again in total darkness, and for a moment I couldn't see. *Where are the lights in this country?* I thought angrily. *Isn't this the capital city of Ukraine?* Then, as my eyes focused, I saw the silhouette of our man heading toward a glimmer of yellow to the right. Ten seconds later, Roger and Matthew were with me, breathing heavily. As we walked together, slowing our pace, the yellow blur became a cluster of taxicabs. The medal salesman had placed our luggage on the ground and was talking to the drivers.

The taxicabs were a civilized sight compared to what we had just seen. Being in a taxi seemed safer than the train station. *Maybe one of the drivers speaks English,* I thought hopefully.

Roger attempted to communicate with the taxi drivers. The only English words they understood were "taxi," "hotel," "center," and "dollar." That was sufficient, however. Roger decided we should go to a hotel in the center of town where someone might speak English. We paid the young man who had helped us three dollars (although he asked for ten), and he disappeared into the darkness.

The taxis were so small that it was impossible to get all of our luggage into just one. We were lucky to fit into only two cabs. Roger was in the first one, and Matt and I followed in the other. As we bounced down the brick streets, our taxi seemed to be going sideways most of the time. "Maybe this is just a bad dream," I told Matthew with my voice quivering from the bumpy ride, "and we will soon wake up."

We had not gone very far until we saw a lighted sign in English that read, "Intourist Hotel." Roger's taxi swerved into the small parking lot, and he went inside. We followed him, pausing just inside the door to watch, hoping that Roger could deliver us from this nightmare. At the desk sat a plump, middle-aged woman with bleached hair. She looked at Roger's distraught face and said in English, "May I help you?"

May you help us? Roger would have gladly fallen at her feet, but he gathered his composure and said politely, "Yes, thank you."

She told him that a hotel room cost $72. Though it seemed expensive to us for a country like Ukraine, we would have paid anything for a room that night. Roger motioned to us to come forward, and we placed our passports on the counter. The blonde woman looked at Matthew and said, "Your son must stay down the hall. Only two guests to a room—hotel policy."

"Oh no! You can't do that!" I pleaded as the lady swept the passports behind the counter. "We have just been through a terrible ordeal. We need to be together."

"We would be very grateful if you would make an exception," Roger said to her, flashing his charming smile.

The lady thought a minute, her face stiff as granite. Without smiling back, the lady turned to Matthew, thrust his passport toward him, lowered her mascara encrusted eyelids and said with her nose in the air, "I never saw you."

Once inside our room, we locked the door. "Safe at last!" Matthew sighed. The room was small but clean. There was no lightbulb in the table lamp, no soap in the shower. There was brown crepe paper for toilet paper, but the dispenser was broken. In the ceiling above the bed was a small, perforated cylinder that mysteriously resembled a microphone. Roger collapsed on the twin bed nearest the window. Matthew headed for the shower. I started looking for the McCammons' phone number. Soon the floor was covered with open suitcases. The address book was in the last bag.

I took a deep breath and dialed the McCammons' number, hoping the telephone system in this country really worked. A strange tone sounded four times and then a recording began to speak. It was George's voice. How comforting to hear an American voice on this side of the world! I left a message telling them where we were, and that we hoped that they hadn't forgotten we were coming. Certainly not!

Twenty minutes later, while Matthew was still in the shower, the phone rang. It was George. He and Toni were so glad that we were safe. They said they had gone to the train station, but their translator had taken them to the wrong track. Even after living in Kiev for six months, George found it difficult to figure out the Ukrainian system. "Since it is so late now, we will pick you up in the morning," he said.

Then Toni came on the phone. "How are Roger and Matthew?" she asked.

"They're fine now. Roger's in bed and Matthew's in the shower," I said.

"Well, be glad you are in the hotel tonight," Toni said, with a humorous sarcasm. "We've not had any hot water for two weeks. We'll see you tomorrow."

What had we gotten ourselves into?

With Matthew finally finished, I took my long awaited shower. The shower had no shower curtain. I stood on a small square platform and squirted myself with a sprayer attached to a metal hose. The warm water felt good flowing down my back, and the tension rolled away as I closed my eyes and relaxed.

Afterward, Matt helped me pull the top mattress from his twin bed to the floor. I moved the suitcases out of the way and positioned it by the open window. I didn't mind sleeping on the floor that night. I was so thankful to have a private bathroom, a warm shower, and a safe place to sleep. It was my first Ukrainian lesson: When uncertainties assail you, simple pleasures are tremendously rewarding.

Chapter 4

A Different World

The next morning George and Toni arrived to retrieve us from the hotel. They carried most of the luggage to their car, and their translator took us by taxi to the apartment that would be our home. It was a typical two-room apartment on the first floor of a three-story building in a large courtyard, whose only entrance was an arched tunnel connecting the courtyard to a main street. In the center of the courtyard was a kindergarten school with a children's playground. During the daytime, one heard the sounds of children playing and birds singing. At night, one heard the homeless dogs barking. Our apartment was located five bus stops from George and Toni's apartment on the same side of the Dnieper River across from the center of town.

The owner of the apartment was a director of a local music school. She had moved in with relatives for five weeks to earn $50 rent for the renovation of her kitchen. The two rooms were long and narrow. The main room was furnished with a bookcase, a couch that converted to a bed at night, and a color television set whose picture was mostly green with a purple spot in the center. The second room had a twin bed and a desk. The bed was short for Matt, but he learned to adjust. A two-room apartment in Ukraine means "two rooms plus a kitchen, a toilet room, and a bath." The kitchen had no cupboards, and all tools were kept on a table. We shared the apartment with a gray cat, which the owner's mother came to feed every day. It insisted on sleeping on our feet at night, until Roger kicked it by accident. Then it kept its distance.

After we had settled into the apartment and rested, George and Toni came to drive the three of us to their place for supper. They lived in a sixteen-story, dirty-white Soviet building next to a small lake. We approached the doorway to the building with foreboding. The white doorway sharply contrasted with the dark hole inside. The stench of rotten cabbage and cat urine welcomed us to the stairwell where prisonlike cement walls and dirty floors led up three broken steps toward the two elevators.

"How can she stand this?" I whispered to Roger as we walked past the sloppily painted metal mailboxes, their numbers indicating the cells where people lived. I smiled falsely into Toni's unaffected face as we waited for the elevator. In her khaki shorts and crisp white blouse, Toni, a bottle of window cleaner in her hand, looked invincible.

The two elevator doors opened simultaneously. We chose to ride in the one that had light. The elevator groaned its way to the ninth floor. When it stopped, the floor button popped out like a gunshot, setting my heart racing. In the hall was broken glass smeared with blood where a drunk had smashed his hand through a frosted glass door. No one had cleaned up the pieces of glass on the floor.

At the end of the hall we came to a black, padded door with a peephole. George gave a special knock, and a voice inside asked, "Who is it?" Then hearing George's voice, the door opened. It was Matthew, the McCammons' son. The two Matthews were glad to see each other.

As we entered the apartment, I was impressed by its spaciousness. There was a center hall with two rooms on either side, providing a pleasant cross breeze. The dining room doubled as an office with stacks of papers covering the table. The living room doubled as Matthew's bedroom, which he had decorated with a large American flag draping one wall. It was the main activity room with an upright piano, television, and a large collection of video tapes. Toni and George's room had a soft double bed and a dresser with a large mirror. Toni's kitchen was small, but she had two refrigerators. Compared to the hall outside, this was paradise.

After a good meal, we took a walk along the lake, which was bordered by six more buildings just like George's in a single row. From there it was a short walk to Music School #20 where we were to hold auditions for our rehearsal accompanist. George's interpreter, Sergei Basarab, was waiting at the entrance.

Sergei was the image of the Ukrainian intellectual. His thick glasses and quiet speech underscored his sensitive personality. Every English phrase was impeccably correct. On Sundays he translated the worship services at George and Toni's church, turning George's English into Ukrainian for the fifty to sixty worshippers there. He was equally fluent in Ukrainian, Russian, or English. His pale skin was a sharp contrast to his black hair, which he combed neatly to one side. Having a deep interest in music and culture, he had already agreed to translate for Roger's rehearsals during our five-week stay.

George's newspaper advertisement for accompanists had brought some results. Two lovely ladies, both named Larisa, arrived to audition. One of them had red hair, and the other had blond hair. It was clear that the older Larisa, with her red hair neatly tied at the back of her neck, had extraordinary skills. She could condense an orchestra score and sight-read perfectly. She was just what we needed for the concert choir.

The blond Larisa, a piano teacher at the music school, would be excellent as the children's choir accompanist that I needed for George's church. I had promised to begin a children's choir for him. This younger Larisa had a sweetness in her soft-spoken manner, and her beautiful blue eyes were eager to please. We named these two ladies "Larisa the Blonde" and "Larisa the Red."

At the end of the auditions, Larisa the Red stayed, and Roger shared with her some of the music he had brought. "Have you ever played this?" he asked, and he placed "Jesu, Joy of Man's Desiring" by Bach on the music rack of the nine-foot grand piano. Larisa began to play, and the beautiful phrases filled the room.

Her whole body was pressing into the keys, and her eyes filled with tears. "No, I've never heard this before. It's wonderful."

Their mutual love of music created a bond that night that went beyond language. Sergei Basarab stayed to translate. He was perhaps the only Ukrainian we met that summer whom we called by his real surname—Basarab. The long Ukrainian names were not only difficult to pronounce but also impossible to remember.

The following evening, with Sergei and Larisa the Red, Roger began the first rehearsal for Handel's *Messiah*. George and Toni had also placed newspaper ads for singers. Forty people showed up for auditions at the College of Communications auditorium downtown. I recorded their names and basic information. Each applicant was a professional singer, anxious to work with this American conductor, learn some interesting new music, and receive a dollar per rehearsal. Rehearsals would be four times a week. Roger accepted thirty-five singers, and Larisa the Blonde, Toni, and I joined the soprano section. I wrote nametags in English letters and took pictures of each person so that we could learn their names.

The chairs in the auditorium were nailed to the floor in long, straight lines, a poor arrangement for ensemble singing. Most of the three-hour rehearsal was spent on the stage where the group could stand in a semicircle to hear each other. A few days later we were able to locate movable chairs, and the stage became our rehearsal room.

The singers loved Roger from the beginning. His enthusiastic style and skillful conducting brought an instant respect and camaraderie. His American manner, accepting them as individuals, created a family atmosphere; soon the solemn expressions at auditions were replaced by smiles and warm greetings as they entered the hall, ready for another rehearsal. "Coming to your rehearsals is like a holiday," one man told him. Laughter was part of the rehearsal, and the choir warmed to every informal comment or personalized reference.

The group gladly devoured the music, learning the notes so quickly that Roger decided to use all the extra music he had brought to do an additional concert. Though pronouncing English was difficult, the group mastered the Latin quickly and worked hard to perfect both.

Sergei was constantly at Roger's elbow, following him around the stage, speaking Russian as quickly as Roger could speak English, almost simultaneously. Larisa the Red played the piano with great artistry. Nothing was too difficult for her. She brought her husband, Stanislav, to audition for the bass solos. His large frame poured out a voice rich as velvet but with a cavernous volume that made your skin tingle. Gruff on the outside, Stanislav sometimes showed tenderness, but one was never sure if he were absolutely tame.

From the photos taken in our first week, it was difficult to identify the singers because their countenances were changing. As we spent time together in those rehearsals, these strangers had become our friends.

To every rehearsal Vera, a chunky lady with round cheeks, brought us apples from her orchard, a snack that could take away our thirst on the hot nights. There was nothing to drink, and we rarely remembered to bring distilled water.

Eugenia, a businesswoman wearing a braid around her head, convinced her boss to print extra copies of the music, if needed, without cost.

Mila, a few years my senior, sat next to me. I became her English teacher. She kept pointing to words, and I would pronounce them for her. When we finished singing a piece for the first time, she would often hug the music to her heart and close her eyes with a low groan of delight. No words were necessary.

Diana with the bright blond hair never missed a rehearsal and listened intently to everything Roger said, especially about God.

Always sitting in the center of the first row with the altos was Valentina, a middle-aged woman, her hair pulled back in a soft Victorian style. Valentina never wore makeup, yet her face, though older, had an innocent glow.

There were five Irinas in the choir, but Irina Loktionova, who spoke very good English, left a stunning impression. She was almost six feet tall with beautiful tan skin and dark brown eyes. Her voice was liquid gold. Even her words sounded like music.

Michael, a poorly dressed middle-aged man, had the manners of a prince. He always greeted me by kissing my hand and saying in English, "Good evening, Deanna." Deanna is my Ukrainian name. From then on, I was no longer called Diane.

At each rehearsal, Roger shared with the choir the historical significance of the music they were singing and clarified the spiritual message of the text. He had always prayed at his rehearsals in America. Roger had asked George, "How do I pray with them when most of them are atheists?" (Even Sergei had admitted to being an atheist.)

"Just treat them as if they are your church choir," advised George. So at the end of each rehearsal, Roger asked them to stand for prayer, which they obediently did. After all, they were getting paid one dollar a rehearsal, a good wage for three hours of work. But as the rehearsals continued, we observed that the people were anxious to pray.

The singers were often amazed by Roger's faith and his perseverance to make things happen. "We are going to perform our concert at the House of Organ and Chamber Music," he said when the Conservatory refused to rent their hall to him. The whole choir broke into laughter. How impossible! Such a large hall with seven hundred seats! Who would come? Yet before the week had ended, the arrangements were made and the posters were printed to advertise the first concert: a program of Bach, Vivaldi, Beethoven, Mozart, and John Rutter's music.

We were having problems with tenors. They just did not read music as quickly as the other sections, and they could not learn the English. One day the entire tenor section did not appear at rehearsal. They had collectively dropped out of the project. "We have an emergency," Roger announced to the choir. "We cannot perform without tenors. We're going to pray and ask God to bring us a whole new tenor section by next rehearsal." He also offered any choir member five dollars for recruiting a tenor of extraordinary talent who would complete the five weeks of singing.

At the next rehearsal we had five new excellent tenors, all of them recruited by one soprano, my friend Mila. The tenors completed our ensemble, and our expectations were high again. These Ukrainians had a new respect for the power of prayer.

In those five weeks, we lived in a simple manner, submerged in a culture we did not fully understand. Though the year was 1992, we felt as if we had been transported back in time fifty years. There were few automobiles, and the signs of poverty were everywhere—broken sidewalks, fields of weeds, an abundance of stray dogs searching garbage dumpsters. A hardware store might have only four items to sell. Among the people we saw so much sadness and very little work.

Though we had brought some food in our suitcase, there were times we had to shop at the market. This was difficult without a translator. I could buy a loaf of bread by pointing and using fingers. But for everything else, such as meat, vegetables, and fruit, I depended on Toni or a translator to go with me to the open market. Unless we went in George's car, it was a forty-minute bus ride with a change of buses. This market, which was the first sign of privatized business in Ukraine, had rows of little wooden tables each managed by a farmer who displayed two kinds of fruits or vegetables. We wandered the aisles, selecting what we needed.

At the rear of the complex was the meat house. Inside were more wooden tables laden with unwrapped pieces of pork or beef for the public to finger through, making their selection. The sound of chopping drew attention to a large tree stump where a man was chopping a large piece of meat with an ax. The cuts of meat looked strange, not as they appear in an American meat market. It was even difficult to know if the meat were pork or beef, but above the table on an iron hook was the clue, either a pig's head or a cow's hoof.

During those five weeks, we lost 15 percent of our body weight. Not only did we have little opportunity to buy food, but we also were almost too busy to eat. We grabbed a granola bar or a Slim-Fast drink in the morning, rarely ate lunch, and left at 5:00 P.M. for rehearsals. We traveled one hour by public transportation to the rehearsal hall and one hour home again. With rehearsals ending at 9:00 P.M., it was impossible to fix supper until 10:30 P.M., and then we were too tired to cook. Macaroni-and-cheese mix was our nightly fast food. We carried eighty pounds of music to the rehearsal in backpacks and handbags every night. There was no safe place to store our music at the hall. We traveled by foot, by bus, by metro, and by foot again up hills and up steps. It did not take us long to shed extra pounds, and our athletic Matthew was becoming a toothpick.

The most frightening moments were walking the dark streets. Every night as we came into the courtyard through the dark tunnel, faceless people were loitering in the shadows. One night a man came running at us, and I grabbed the mace in my purse. But all he wanted was a light for his cigarette. It was several weeks until I no longer felt panic in the dark.

In the morning we saw children at the kindergarten, sunlight and trees, people walking quickly along the boulevard, each one carrying a bag to collect the day's food or supplies. Old women wore bedroom slippers instead of shoes because they could afford nothing else. Three mornings a week, I would attempt to get on Bus #3. By the third bus, I usually squeezed into the crowd as the doors slammed behind me. I was headed for Music School #20 where I held children's choir rehearsals for George's church with the help of Larisa the Blonde at the piano. I loved working with the kids. They so wanted to learn songs in English, and I used a translator to communicate with them.

Most mornings the buses were jammed with people. It was not unusual to have four different bodies pressed against your own. Once I dropped an earring. There was no hope to recover it. Throw the other one away and forget it. Even if I knew the Russian word for earring, no one could help me. No one could move.

At the children's choir rehearsals, I became friends with two sisters, Bogdana and Oksana. They were teenagers in George's church and had some musical training. Both girls could lead a section reading three-part music. The older sister, Bogdana, spoke some English, and we were able to communicate quite well. She was sixteen years old, but had an innocence that made her seem younger. Because she enjoyed playing the piano, she asked on several occasions if she could take the music home. One day I asked Bogdana if she would again like to borrow some music to play at home. She said, "Oh, no, Mrs. Deanna. It is not necessary. I have already copied all the vocal and instrumental parts on my notepaper."

We learned many musical pieces that summer, enough to give a concert at the end of the five weeks at the church. With the help of Oksana and Bogdana, I was able to conduct a teenage ensemble performing three-part music, in addition to my work with the general children's choir. Being with the young people was tremendously fulfilling as I was able to share about God and my personal faith. I knew that God was using me in a significant way with these beautiful children, who were so open to discovering and experiencing the Lord.

One night Roger, Matthew, and I were leaving the McCammons' building, and we gazed at the moon. "Matthew," said Roger, with his arm on his shoulder, "that's the same moon that is shining in America. Amazing, isn't it?"

"Yeah! If I saw five moons here, I wouldn't be surprised," replied Matthew.

And that's how it felt. We felt as if we were on another planet. We had stepped into another world that was, in some ways, familiar but with a strange twist. It was unlike anything we had experienced before, not as in Europe, not as the Orient. Soviet-style living was oppressive and covered the city like a dark cloud. Yet freedom was dawning, however faintly, in Ukraine. Our Ukrainian friends did not yet realize what that meant. As Americans, we modeled that spirit of freedom in our smiles, our music, and our Christian witness. We were beating down the cobwebs of the past and pointing toward an open door whose portals were inscribed with the words, "The Truth shall make you free."

Chapter 5

Larisa the Red and Larisa the Blonde

During the five weeks we were in Kiev, we had little time for recreation. We did visit a few homes of our new Ukrainian friends, however. Two memorable evenings were with our two Larisas.

Larisa the Red invited us to a party at her home following the first concert. The soloists were there; her husband Stanislav, who had mesmerized the audience with "Deep River"; and their two daughters, Sophia and Nastia. Sophia, eleven years old, was a brilliant young musician already composing her own music on the piano. Nastia, a short name for Anastasia, was nine. Both girls were stunningly beautiful with shiny blond hair.

The girls helped their mother bring food to the table, which was not an easy task. The family lived in a two-story apartment on the top two floors of a large apartment building downtown. The kitchen, bath, and girls' bedroom were on the first level connected by a long hall cluttered with children's shoes and old bicycles. There were two rooms upstairs including a formal room that housed a German Steinway. Larisa said she had bought the piano years ago for thirteen dollars' worth of rubles. This was the room where Larisa taught music and guests were entertained. The girls ran up and down the stairs from the kitchen to the main room, carrying plates of food which they graciously offered to their guests.

This was my first visit to Larisa and Stanislav's home. Roger had spent many afternoons there working with the soloists and Larisa. Roger told me that one day Larisa and the girls had invited him to use their shower, which Stanislav had built on a large patio outside the first level. When Roger realized that the shower had no curtain and was visible from all the windows of the house, he felt too uncomfortable to accept.

Whenever he visited Larisa's apartment, she insisted on cooking for him. He resisted, saying he didn't need any food, but she brought him potatoes and meat or hot soup from her kitchen. One night they worked until evening. It had been a long day, and Roger was very tired. He gave Stanislav a dollar and asked if he would walk him to the street to get him a taxi. When they reached the boulevard, Stanislav put the dollar in his pocket and pulled him onto a bus, accompanying him all the way home. He just couldn't see spending an entire dollar on a taxi ride. Then Stanislav kept the dollar.

Stanislav had been trained as a carpenter in his youth. He worked in a factory for several years, but then he discovered that he had a wonderful bass voice and started singing. He became a soloist at the Children's Opera Theater, where he played the role of kings and powerful male heroes. His name was Stanislav Pavlenko. His girls carried his name, but Larisa was known as Larisa Reutova. She was a star musician herself, and everyone called her by her professional name. Because of the exclusiveness of the Pavlenkos' apartment, Roger suspected that Stanislav must have had some powerful position in the Soviet government. So much room was not normal for a musician's family. Many musicians lived in this building, but no one had as much space as Stanislav. I was somewhat afraid of him. Roger said he had a vicious temper. When the three of them worked together on Stanislav's solos, Larisa would try to help Stanislav and he would yell at her unmercifully.

Larisa was one of the hardest workers we met in Ukraine. Whether it was coaching soloists, playing rehearsals, cooking for guests, or negotiating schedules, she always gave herself 100 percent to the task. I loved watching her play the piano. The intensity in her eyes fascinated me. Though she had worked all day in rehearsals and played in the concert, she was now cooking potatoes and cutting sausages and bread. Cans of smoked fish were opened, and soon the table was full of food as well as a variety of drinks.

The table was slightly larger than a coffee table, and ten of us sat around it. Roger, Matthew, Sergei our translator, and I were given the place of honor on the couch. The other guests—soloists and invited friends—sat on stools and straight-backed chairs.

We talked about music and politics. We learned much about the backgrounds and lives of the musicians present. Sergei got very little to eat that night. His mouth was constantly interpreting for someone who wanted to communicate to the Americans. They wanted us to know how they felt about their lives, and their stories were fascinating.

When we looked at our watches, we realized that it was very late. "You must hurry to catch the last subway train," said Sergei. Everyone left quickly. The little girls gave us warm hugs and said, "I love you" in English. We went as one group to the metro and said goodbye at various stops as each one departed for home. Finally Roger, Matt, and I were riding alone. We were the only ones to cross the river.

By the time we arrived at our metro stop and were on the street, we noticed that the buses had stopped running. We were five miles from home without transportation. It was almost two o'clock in the morning. We started walking. After stumbling several times in the dark over the broken sidewalks, we started walking in the street. The three of us argued about which street would take us home. They all looked alike. We knew that the bus took two turns. Were we going the right way?

A car passed us every five minutes. Gathering his courage, Roger stood with Matthew under a lonely street light and held out a dollar bill. I kept walking, hoping no one would stop. Too dangerous, I thought. Finally a junky East German car pulled over for the dollar. Roger motioned me to the car and I reluctantly followed. *"Leningrad Ploshet,"* Roger said, naming the intersection nearest our home. I repeated it through the open window. And Matthew said it after we did. We knew we had to pronounce it correctly to get home. The driver, a young man about twenty, looked at us blankly, then nodded and motioned for us to get in. "Mr. Sandman" with the McGuire Sisters was blaring from his radio. In 1992, they were still playing 1950s music. In ten minutes, he brought us to our destination, and we walked the rest of the way.

Our experience at the home of Larisa the Blonde was quite different. We were invited for "tea" with George, Toni, their son Matthew, and Sergei. George told us, "If they said 'tea,' don't eat anything all day."

Larisa lived at the end of Bus Line 45 on our same side of the river. Roger and Sergei decided to ride the bus because there was room for only five people in George's car. Not knowing exactly where Bus 45 went, we followed their bus, breathing in its smoky exhaust all the way. The journey ended in a city of high-rise buildings that all looked alike. Each building had a number, neither clearly visible nor in numerical order. We followed Roger and Sergei, who searched on foot, and finally located Larisa's building, where we parked the car.

The apartment building looked fairly new. The stairwell was not nearly as dark and dirty as the one George and Toni had. After climbing five flights of stairs (there was no elevator), we found the right door. Larisa was glad to see us. Her long blond hair flowed over the shoulders of her white dress. She looked like an angel. Her mother, Paulina, also blond, wore a long silver dress beautifully accented by dangling earrings. Her father, Leonard, and brother, Roman, wore short-sleeved sport shirts. Neither could speak a word of English, but they bowed slightly when introduced.

We entered the main room through a curtain of glass beads. The apartment was much smaller than Larisa the Red's, but it was attractively decorated and very neat. In the center of the room was a lace covered table with a vase of red roses, elegant crystal, and tiered plates of freshly cut fruit. I complimented Paulina on her beautiful table. "We used to have nice things," she replied. "But who knows the future?"

Paulina and Larisa carried more plates of food to the table: smoked fish, salami, beef or salmon on mini-slices of bread, pastry topped with tomato or cucumber, and egg wedges, all attractively decorated with sprigs of green. We were invited to sit at the table. It was a larger table than the one at Larisa the Red's home. Sitting in front of the fresh flowers and elegant dinnerware, I felt as if we were in Europe.

In our conversation, we discovered that Paulina and Leonard had been scientists assigned to Chernobyl. They were in the nearby village when the nuclear explosion happened in 1988. They saw it from their window, less than two miles from the reactor. Fortunately Larisa was absent from the region at the time. Few people knew about the disaster of Chernobyl or its significance immediately after the accident. Paulina and Leonard knew, but they were helpless to do anything about it. Two days later in Kiev, thousands of Ukrainians and their children celebrated May Day outside in the open air, not knowing that the invisible poison was falling upon them.

The Soviet government moved Larisa's family seventy miles from Chernobyl, relocating them in Kiev. They were not happy in Kiev. They were Russian, not Ukrainian, and they felt trapped now that the Soviet Union had fallen and Ukraine was an independent country. Their surname was Toporkova. Names in Eastern Europe reveal a person's heritage, whether Russian, Ukrainian, or Jewish. Everyone knew they were Russian. They had been part of the elite scientific group there. Now they had no choice about where they lived.

Leonard did not look well, and I wondered if his paleness was the effect of Chernobyl. "You are the first Americans we have ever met," he said. "We never dreamed we would be sitting around this table with our former enemies, eating together and speaking freely. This is like a fairy tale. Even when we toured Germany, we were told to stay with our Russian group and not to talk to Americans."

"How did you feel about that?" Toni asked.

"We felt insulted, yet we thought it was what we should do," he replied with downcast eyes.

George asked if we could pray before we began the meal. Leonard said with a wistful look in his eye, "We used to pray to Lenin. To whom do we pray now?"

Paulina, his wife, immediately responded, "Yes, why don't you pray for us?" We bowed our heads, and as George prayed, Sergei translated his prayer.

From this point the conversation turned to the future and God. Paulina said, "We are atheists. We have always been taught atheism. But now I wonder about God. I know very little about the Bible."

Then her husband interrupted, "How can people who have been atheists for so long ever know God? Why would He want to know them?"

I shared with them how I came to know Christ and ended by saying, "That you think about God, and wonder how you might know him is a good thing. It might be that he is calling to you and wants you to know him. When you know Jesus, you need not fear the future or even death."

Our son Matthew shared about his faith in God and the comfort of belonging to the Lord. Then Roger shared how his father was raised in an atheist home, but when he heard of Christ at the age of fourteen, he became a Christian and later became a pastor. Roger said, "God freely offers his forgiveness to anyone who will come to him." Sensing their continued interest, he asked, "Do you have a Bible in your home?"

Larisa got up from the table. "Yes, I have one," she said. She brought a Russian Bible from her room and gave it to Sergei.

Roger asked him read from Isaiah 55. "Read the beginning of the chapter," he said. Sergei began to read in the Russian language:

Come, all you who are thirsty, come to the waters;
and you who have no money, come, buy and eat!

Since Roger did not tell him where to stop, he kept reading. I did not know word for word what was being read, but at one point I saw something in Larisa's face that made me want to stop Sergei and say: What are those words? But he stopped reading right after that. So later, in private, I asked him, "What was the last verse that you read?"

"Verse five," he said. What he had read was this:

Surely you will summon nations you know not,
and nations that do not know you will hasten to you,
because of the Lord your God, the Holy One of Israel,
for He has endowed you with splendor.

I remembered that verse for a long time to come. It reminded me of the opportunity we had to share Christ with people who spoke another language. Yet they responded with such openness and interest. It could happen only through the working of the Holy Spirit.

After the dinner, Leonard invited us to sit on the couch and look at their family photo albums. There were some pictures of Larisa's childhood and Chernobyl where they had lived. Then we returned to the table, which was now filled with desserts. I wondered how I could take another mouthful, but I wanted to be polite. This family had given us their best in every way. We no longer felt like strangers.

We parted with many hugs. They followed us down the stairway and hugged us again before we crowded into George's car. Sergei opted to walk to the nearby bus stop since he was going another direction.

Before we left, Larisa told George that she wanted to come to his church and help Toni with the children's classes. We drove away with a greater understanding of how the Ukrainians lived, grateful for the opportunity to speak about God with them.

Larisa the Blonde came to church the following Sunday. That morning, I was scheduled to give my testimony. I shared my personal story about how I met Jesus Christ as my Savior and Lord. Larisa told me afterward in Russian, "Your words tugged at my heart." She and I had been working together, teaching songs about the Lord with the children's choir for three weeks, but now I hoped that Larisa was on a spiritual journey of her own that would continue long after I left Kiev.

Larisa the Red came to the church only a few times, but after we left Kiev, her daughters joined the children's choir I had begun. Sometimes Sophia, the elder daughter, would accompany them on the piano. Stanislav even came a few times to sing a solo in worship. A month after we left, the girls were baptized in the Dnieper River by George McCammon. Another chapter in the book of "Changed Lives" began.

Chapter 6

Premier Concerts

A s the calendar turned from July to August, we had ten days
left in Kiev and two concerts to present. On August 2, Roger's
choir performed the first concert featuring short pieces of famous
classical composers. The Dome Organi Musiki, which had been a
Polish Catholic cathedral until the Communists turned it into a
concert hall, was filled with people anxious to see what this American conductor would do with Ukrainian musicians. For the very
first time, the audience heard a variety of Western music from
Mozart's "Gloria in Excelsis" to "When the Saints Go Marchin' In."
One of the finest orchestras in Ukraine, the Kiev Philharmonic,
joined the choir in this presentation.

With the success of the first concert, the enthusiasm escalated
toward the grand performance of Handel's Messiah. This performance would be our last night in Ukraine. Our Ukrainian singers
had become our dear friends. At the last choir rehearsal (Roger's
birthday), they surprised him with gifts of flowers, songs, and a
glowing tribute written from their hearts. In her golden voice, Irina
Loktionova read the English words:

> You can't imagine how many minutes of happiness and real plea-
> sure you have brought us. You have changed our lives so that
> we forgot all our troubles and entered the world of joy and beauty.
> It was you who led us during these unforgettable weeks to the
> universe of music as well as to the inaccessible dwelling of God.
> We believe you so much and try to penetrate the beauty of the

great creations of the human mind, and to experience the mercy and kindness of the Lord. We tried to improve our skills and do our best to magnify worthily the sacred name of God. We shall pray for you and your family and shall be waiting to see you soon. God be with you!

Their lives had been changed, they said, and they had entered into a new world. God was changing them, indeed, and through His music they beheld Him. The door to understanding had been unlocked, and the spiritual journey for many was beginning according to His purpose and plan.

The following afternoon Roger met the orchestra again, this time for the *Messiah* rehearsal. During the first playing of the "Hallelujah Chorus," Roger saw tears in the eyes of the concertmaster. When they had finished, Roger asked the orchestra, "Have you ever played this before?" No one had. "Have you ever *heard* it before?" Again the sad response was no. These brilliant artists had been denied access to this great music, but now they thrilled to play it with technical excellence and deep feeling. When the five-hour rehearsal concluded, the concertmaster stood up and spoke for the group. "May we rehearse another hour? We want to perfect this music. It will not cost any more money to do so." Though exhausted from his work, Roger agreed, amazed at their dedication to their art.

The next day was the *Messiah* concert. The hall was overflowing with expectant faces. The printed program, containing the entire biblical text of *Messiah* in Ukrainian, was distributed to all. The room was warm, and the orchestra, dressed in white shirts and no jackets, took their places. They had come two hours earlier that day for yet another rehearsal, which they had requested, not because they were lacking in proficiency but because they wanted perfection. The choir filled the steps behind them. Then Roger entered with the soloists, and the room burst into applause. As Roger turned toward the musicians, the room grew instantly quiet.

Like healing salve, the glorious sounds of the first few chords of the overture poured over the audience. Then the first words were tenderly sung, "'Comfort ye! Comfort ye, my people!' saith your God."

In this dark cathedral—stolen from the Catholic church by the Communists, where God had been ignored, denied, and profaned for seventy years—the words of His Scripture were being sung. That night something extraordinarily profound happened. The message of *Messiah* was the message for Ukraine, a spiritually and economically impoverished land. Though this had been the birthplace of Christianity for all of Eastern Europe, its churches had been burned, its priests murdered, and its people oppressed. The song continued, "Your warfare is over. Your iniquity is pardoned."

Later the powerful bass resonance in Stanislav's voice filled the cathedral, proclaiming, "The people that walked in darkness have seen a great Light." It was beyond words or music. The reality of the darkness, the comfort of the Light. The only word that could adequately describe it was "splendor."

During the "Hallelujah Chorus," my voice choked with emotion as I tried to sing, "The kingdom of this world is become the kingdom of our Lord and of His Christ." The tyranny of Communism was over. Freedom was here. God had brought this to pass for His glory. I had sung the *Messiah* many times, but singing to those upturned faces so longing for hope was an experience I will never forget.

The people in the audience did not forget it either. Years later Edward Senko, a teacher of conducting at the Tchaikovsky Conservatory, told me, "That evening I was seated in the audience and all I could feel was Light. I knew I had to be near that Light."

In that dark cathedral, the Light was dawning in Ukraine.

Chapter 7

Saying Goodbye

The *Messiah* concert finalized our stay in Kiev. After the performance, we said our farewells to the singers and our other friends. Larisa the Blonde said to me, "I wish you would not go."

"We will be back," I promised her. We had already decided to come back next summer. "If we don't go away, we can't bring you all the music we want to share with you." She looked at me as though she did not believe we would return.

Toni and I had chosen Anna, one of the altos, to direct the children's choir I had trained. Although she did not speak English, Anna was a sensitive person and brilliant musician who would work well with children. I prayed that the children's choir program would continue. Bogdana and Aksana said they would help, and Larisa the Blonde said she would continue to accompany.

The next morning we were packing our suitcases to go home to America. I picked up the jacket with the world map on it, looked at the region that had been so foreign to me, and said to myself with a melancholy sigh, "Now I know where Ukraine is."

Five weeks had seemed like an eternity when we first settled into this apartment. At first I had been counting the days until we would return to America. Now it was time to leave, but something inside me said, "Stay!" I would not miss the frustrations of living in Ukraine, but I was already missing the people.

When the time came, George drove us to the train station. At the front entrance of the terminal, we were surprised to see some friends who had come to say goodbye. Anna had brought a basket with a cooked chicken wrapped in a linen cloth. Vera was holding a sack of apples. Stanislav was there with his two daughters who smothered us with hugs and kisses. Sergei stood beside them with a wistful look in his eye.

Accompanying us to the train, the group insisted on carrying our luggage and coming aboard. The food they brought would last the twenty-five hour trip to Budapest. Carrying the heaviest suitcase, Stanislav was the first person into the compartment. His massive frame filled half of the standing space. As the others handed the suitcases full of music to him, he swung them to the overhead shelf. Sergei tried to come inside to help, but his slender form got caught between Stanislav and the door frame. "Ex-squeeze me!" whined Sergei, half in good humor, half in frustration.

We took time to say goodbye to each person in the narrow hallway of the train. One by one they left. Anna was crying. The girls hung on our necks. Then only Stanislav was left. He gave us each a bear hug and a look of desperation. He just stood there, not wanting to leave. Suddenly the train jerked and started to move forward. Roger said gently, "Stanislav, you'd better get off the train." He lingered a moment more, then turned, and jumped off the moving car.

As the train pulled away, I leaned my head out the window, waving back at the group on the platform and snapping pictures. They were walking quickly, following us. Anna was really crying now, and her eyes were red. Stanislav was jogging from the rear, gaining on the group. The two little girls were leading the way. But Stanislav, like a wild buffalo, passed everyone by. As the platform ended, he stopped, raised his big hand in the air, and with his head tilted to one side, waved farewell.

Our hearts were tied to that little group huddled on the platform, but all too soon the distance took them from our sight.

Chapter 8

The Call

The three of us came through the "time zone" to the other side. Budapest, which had looked so dreary on the way toward Kiev, now seemed modern and bright. The train to Munich was extraordinarily clean and luxurious to our eyes. Then, after many hours of air travel, we finally landed in the United States.

We told many people about our experiences and our desire to go again next summer. One of the first things we did was to gather contributions from our friends to send *Messiah* scores to the Kiev singers. I glued the photo of an American donor inside each cover, hoping to create a friendship between Americans and Ukrainians, and we shipped them to Kiev for Christmas. Matthew, Roger, and I spoke of Kiev often to each other, and we were continually amazed by the size of American cars, private houses, and manicured lawns, as if we were seeing them from Ukrainian eyes.

Two weeks later I was sitting in the church choir loft in the worship service. Every time we would sing about missions or any song that had the word "world" in it, I choked on the words, overcome with an emotion that was hard to explain. I could not erase the faces of our Ukrainians from my mind.

Our house, which had seemed perfect, was now too large for our needs, and the mortgage payment, too excessive for our consciences. We decided to put the house on the market. I knew God wanted us to sell it, but I didn't know exactly why.

In October, Roger was invited to lead the music at a Legonier Bible conference in San Diego. I decided to go too. Because I had accumulated some free airline miles, we would fly separate airlines.

My flight was not crowded. I sat alone next to the window, looking at the puffy white clouds below. *The world looks small and simple from here,* I thought. *Lord, my problems always seem small when I look at the largeness of Your creation.* Then I opened my Bible to Isaiah 55 and began to read. It was the same chapter Sergei had read at Larisa the Blonde's home in Kiev.

"Come, all you who are thirsty, come to the waters . . ."

What a comforting thought. God invites us to come to those still waters that refresh and nourish us.

As I read on, I had a distinct sensation of the presence of God, and every word was a message full of meaning to me.

"Why should you spend money on what does not satisfy?"

Since we had returned to America, we had felt restless. All was well, but all was empty. I had everything, yet I had nothing. I felt as if life in America was not real anymore, and I was detached from everything around me.

Then the fifth verse spoke to me with a command so powerful that it almost took my breath away.

> Surely you will summon nations you know not,
> and nations that do not know you will hasten unto you,
> because of the Lord your God, the Holy One of Israel,
> for He has endowed you with splendor.

And then I knew! I knew we were going to Ukraine—not for a summer but for much longer. How much longer? I had no idea. I knew only that it was real and I had to go—the details would come later. Regardless of the absurdity of the idea, I felt at peace about it.

When the plane landed and I met Roger, I wondered what he would say about this. Would he laugh at me? Would he say that my mind is playing tricks? I kept silent all the way to the hotel, knowing that I needed to tell him, yet waiting for the right moment. Finally, alone in the hotel room, I was about to broach the subject when he said to me, "Diane, I had a strange experience on the plane. I know that God wants us to move to Ukraine, and I promised Him that I would go."

I was shocked, yet not as surprised as he looked when I said, "I had the same experience." I recounted to him how God had spoken to me in that scripture. Now we felt scared and excited at the same time. As we talked further in the privacy of that room, we knew God's call was real, and we were ready to go. We also knew that our lives would never be the same.

We called our son Matthew first. If we were going, he, at fifteen years old, needed to go with us. What would he say? He was speechless at first, but then he said, "I'm going. Even if you two don't go, I'm going anyway."

Then we called George and Toni in Kiev. George's response was: "If God is calling you, we'll move heaven and earth to get you here."

Everything was moving too fast. My head was spinning. If we moved to Ukraine, we would have to leave everything behind—sell the house, the car, and everything in the house just to be debt free. Visa card and all credits accounts would have to be emptied. We would leave a comfortable, full-time church music position—no more health insurance, no more retirement, no more secure income.

How would we live? If the sale of our belongings went well, we might survive on our own in Kiev for six weeks. What then? We did not know the answer,

The next day at breakfast with a group of ministers, Roger confided to a friend, "Archie, I think the Lord is calling me to Ukraine, and I'm scared." Archie, knowing about our summer trip there, said matter-of-factly, "Well, Roger, I'm scared for you if you *don't* go."

The theme of the conference was "Rescued from Wrath": We cannot fully appreciate the value of our salvation until we fully understand what we have been rescued *from*. Lecture after lecture confirmed in my spirit the need to take the message of the gospel to Ukraine. Without the gospel, these people, who had been under the curse of atheistic Communism, would perish. I wanted to begin today.

Even though the need was urgent, we also knew that we had obligations to fulfill. It was not fair to leave our church without sufficient notice, enabling them to find a replacement. Roger had planned a "killer" year with many concerts, a major musical, and four summer choir tours (one to Canada, one to Washington, DC, and two to Europe). We needed to finish what we had begun.

A week later in Orlando, we went to our boss and pastor, Dr. Edington. He greeted us at his home in a plaid short-sleeved shirt, his blond hair neatly combed to the side. He knew for us to come there on a Monday meant something important. The news we shared with him brought a mixed reaction. He rejoiced in our calling but cautioned us to be prudent, saying that, for the good of the church and the people we loved there, we should not announce our plans too early. It could start a grief process at a time when we wanted to finish a year of fully planned activities. Long goodbyes are painful. We agreed to wait until after Easter Sunday, another seven months.

With the question of our future settled, we could now fully pour ourselves into our work, making the most of our final year in church music. We loved the people in the church intensely as we realized we would soon have to say goodbye. The choirs excelled beyond our dreams as we performed the *St. Matthew Passion* with adults, orchestra, and professional ballet. The youth choirs gave performances of *The King and I* that would rival any professional troupe.

In March I packed some items, including our king-sized bed, a twin bed for Matt, a file cabinet, a computer, and a card table as well as kitchen supplies and books, and sent them in a container by ship to the McCammons in Kiev. Though we had shared our plans with some friends outside of Orlando, we still had not told most of our friends about our decision. By the time the announcement came at church, we were almost to summer touring season. Six weeks remained until our departure, June 24.

Then we had a chance for a safety net. It was a good idea in the world's view. Why jump in with both feet when you can test the waters? The church offered us a leave of absence for a year, so that if we discovered we had made a grave error, we could return to our jobs. We knew in our hearts that God's call was absolutely clear, however. We waived the offer. We also knew that to accept it would hurt the church, delaying the new program that must begin with a new director.

By June the house had not sold. Roger and I left on tour to Canada, realizing that if the house did not sell, we could not leave for Ukraine. Before the end of the month, the church offered to buy our house as a parsonage for the new youth pastor, and they took over our mortgage.

We hired two ladies to manage the sale of our belongings. They put a price tag on everything in our house except for two vases Roger had given me and a few furniture pieces that we gave to Matthew and our older, married son Marc. "Everything must go— furniture, paintings, books, knickknacks, clothes—and whatever doesn't sell, just give it away," I said. Three days before we left for Ukraine, everything was gone.

I had forgotten to rescue my cedar chest from the garage before it was whisked off to a charity organization. Inside the chest was my wedding dress, the outfits my two baby sons wore when they were baptized, and some memory artwork from their preschool years. At first I felt terrible. I kept replaying in my mind what I could have done to keep these precious things. It was more than money. They were important pieces of my life!

But I must let go of it all! I didn't really need things anymore. I must empty my hands if I expected God to bring new blessings.

Finally I came to terms with letting go. It was with a sense of relief that I looked at the empty house. All those things that I spent so much energy accumulating, cleaning, and managing were gone. A freedom swept into my soul, and I actually felt happy about it.

The most difficult part of letting go was to leave family. Our older son, Marc, his wife and two young sons—were a family struggling to survive economically. But now they would have to struggle without Mom and Dad nearby. I remembered the day Marc and Sharilyn were married, the day their first son Taylor was born, and the joy we had at holiday times. Young Cody was less than a year old. We would not see them grow up. We would not have a gathering place for family where they could come, do laundry, and chat over the kitchen table or play basketball in the driveway.

Roger's eighty-six-year-old widowed mother shed tears at the news, yet she told Roger how he was fulfilling her dream. She had always wanted to be a missionary. How happy his father would have been, had he known. Dad McMurrin had been a pastor and had had such a heart for the lost.

My mother tried to be brave, but I knew I was leaving an emotional void in her heart by walking out the door, and I felt guilty about it. "When are you coming back for good?" she asked. "I don't know," I told her honestly. "Roger says in ten years, maybe."

Matthew had to leave his girlfriend, Maraya. They had known each other for three years and were inseparable, at least by telephone. I took him to her house for a final ten-minute farewell. As we drove to the airport from there, I was not prepared for the level of grief he displayed. At first it was a quiet weeping, but then he burst into wailing as if he were being torn in two. With my hands on the steering wheel, I could not attempt to comfort him, except with my voice. I didn't know what to say to him. The intensity of his grief frightened me. My heart ached for him, and I remembered a similar scene:

It was his thirteenth birthday. We had just moved to Orlando. He had left his friends whom he had known since the age of four. We were moving him from a Christian school to an overcrowded public school where he knew no one. It was his third day, and he did not want to go. He was begging me with tears not to take him to this school. My heart ached for him as we drove across town. We could not go back to the past, and we had to face the future. It was a miserable year for him, but he worked through it. The experience had made him stronger. Still, I had wanted to take the hurt for him, but I could not.

Now sixteen, Matt was sacrificing far more than I was. It is a fearsome thing to move a teenager from place to place in America, let alone to a country like Ukraine. I had the security of my relationship with Roger, but he would have to make new friends who did not speak his language. A few might speak English. Yet he never doubted that the Lord was calling us to Kiev as a family.

Matthew and I knew it would be six months until we would visit America again. God graciously cushioned our path to Kiev with American friends. First we flew to Munich with members of our adult choir, where we began a concert tour in churches throughout northern Germany. During that tour we received news that our last housekeeping task, the selling of our car, had been completed in the States, one day before the insurance expired.

Two weeks later Roger returned to Orlando with the adult choir and gathered the high school choir for the next European tour. Matthew and I stayed with friends in Germany and awaited his friends. The high school group brought many extra suitcases full of music and supplies that we would need in Kiev. The teenagers gave concerts in southern Germany and Switzerland. By the end of July, we bid goodbye to them at the Munich airport. Still we were not alone. Three teenagers, three adults, and Toni and Matthew McCammon were accompanying us through Budapest and on the same Soviet train back to Kiev. With forty pieces of luggage, we headed east, back to the country to which we had been called. Our six American friends would be with us for two and a half weeks, until we had given the first concert in Kiev, in which they would participate.

What would we do once the concert was over? We would wait upon the Lord, but we would not be idle. George and Toni needed volunteer teachers for their new school, St. Andrew's Preparatory School. I would teach high school English, and Roger would teach music theory and world history. In exchange for our work, Matt would receive free tuition and have two additional teachers in the high school of four students studying correspondence courses from the University of Nebraska.

Roger wanted to continue to do more concerts, but we didn't know how this would be possible. We had spent all our savings on last summer's concerts. From the house sale we had funds to do one more while our American friends were there. We knew there were choir members in Kiev awaiting our return. With Larisa the Red and Sergei Basarab, we would begin again. We knew only that God had called us, and we were going to Ukraine!

Chapter 9

The Arrival in Kiev

The arrival at the Kiev train station felt very different the second time. It was dark, but we were not alone. One by one, we climbed off the train wagon: Roger, Matthew, and I, followed by Toni McCammon and her son Matthew, who had been singing on the tour with us. George was there to meet us with a big smile. Now the other Americans climbed from the train. Roger's brother Dwight, a fifty-eight-year-old school teacher, was physically impaired with a fused spine from a polio operation. This trip had not been easy for him with all the walking that was required. Next was a retired couple, Maynard and Nancy Sikes, choir member friends from the church. Finally three teenagers appeared—Blair, Bradley, and Larry—Matt's choir friends who came along for the adventure.

We were surprised to see a Ukrainian man approaching with a small wagon—a baggage cart. *This* certainly was an improvement! We piled most of the forty suitcases onto the cart and followed it to the parking lot. George had hired a bus to pick up our group, but the Mafia-controlled taxi service had forced it to stay outside the area. We took our luggage from the cart, carried it another five minutes to our bus, which was waiting under a distant tree. When I arrived, some of George's workers were loading the suitcases brigade-style into the bus.

George had arranged housing for our group in four separate apartments. Our apartment, which had been George's old office, would be the first stop. The sparsely furnished flat was waiting, filled with the many boxes we had shipped from America. When these belongings first arrived, George had hired a man with a gun to sleep on top of our boxes in a warehouse.

It was midnight when the bus stopped outside the building of our new home, and we dragged the suitcases onto the narrow street, designed more for walking than for vehicles. We entered the stairwell in absolute darkness. With the aid of a flashlight, we found the small elevator and began piling suitcases into it. Anxious to see my new home, I climbed the stairs in the dark to the fifth floor. As I approached the landing, the light from our apartment spilled through the open door, revealing the silhouette of a huge, black dog. For a moment I was frozen with fear. The dog, standing motionless, would not let me come up the steps. Finally his owner, who had been guarding our apartment, came and took him inside, and I walked through the door.

Though I had been in the apartment before, I felt as if I were seeing it for the first time.

It was primitive. The wooden floors were gray with dirt and had no polish or finished coating on them. The wallpaper was pea-green with white patches where it had been torn from the wall.

Near the entrance were two closet doors: one to the toilet and one to the tub and sink room. There was barely enough room to squeeze between the tub and the wall. The sink had a long faucet that swiveled above the tub so it could service both. The toilet room was wallpapered with one coupon Ukrainian currency bills. In eighteen months the "coupon" had been devalued from fifty cents to one-tenth of a cent because of inflation. George's employee had wallpapered these in protest.

The next door in the hall led to the kitchen, which measured seven feet by nine feet, and had a small refrigerator, a small gas stove, a midget-sized corner sink, and a folding table. Above the sink was the only wall cupboard, with an additional lower cupboard between the sink and the stove, its door hanging crookedly ajar. The bottom half of the walls was covered with blue and black wall tiles. The wallpaper above them was two different shades of brown. I was standing in the hallway ready to explore the other three rooms when I heard the elevator door open and voices in the stairwell.

Dwight walked through the door from the darkness outside, looked at me, and said in amazement, "You're not going to *live* here, are you?"

"It's not so bad," I said, trying to be cheerful. "It just needs some fixing up." Dwight turned away so I could not see his tears. Matt, Bradley, and Larry came in with their suitcases. They would be staying with us in our apartment. Dwight left with George, and the bus took the other Americans to their accommodations.

The six of us set up our quarters in the three remaining rooms. Matt assembled his twin bed in the smallest room next to the kitchen. Bradley and Larry took the living room with its pea-green wallpaper. It was furnished with a large breakfront, a brown lacquered folding table, and six straight-backed chairs plus a couch that made into a small double bed. Larry took the couch, and Bradley inflated an air mattress on the dirty floor. We found our king-sized bed unassembled in the farthest room, which opened directly onto the living room. We were extremely tired. I opened a box marked "bedroom" and found some sheets. We spread them over the mattress and collapsed onto it. Surrounded by stacks of cardboard boxes, we fell asleep, trusting that everything would look better in the morning.

Chapter 10

Getting Started

The next day we attempted to clean the apartment. The more we swept the floor, the more dirt appeared. We were sure that it was coming from between the floors through the floorboards. Finally we developed a system of wet mopping every day with large sponges. The boys hated the job, but they did it. We served meals for our American group of five adults and four teenagers every day. This lasted for two and a half weeks, while the group helped us fix up the apartment and also rehearsed with the choir for the first concert.

That week we held the first meeting of our choir. Almost everyone returned from the previous summer. Though we had invited only thirty five people, fifty came to the third-floor room of the Polytechnical Institute where we practiced. Their friends had come to audition, and each one was extraordinarily talented. In order to prepare the concert in only eighteen days, we rehearsed five nights a week. "Music Helen," George's choir director at the church, conducted a choir there during the day, and she arranged for us to have the room in the evenings, rent free. The room did not have enough chairs for fifty people, so most of the singers sat on boards supported by chairs with broken backs. Even so, some singers had to stand for the three-hour rehearsal. Because there was no locked area to store our music there, the six Americans helped us carry the music to and from rehearsals in backpacks and small suitcases.

Stanislav joined the rehearsals too, although his voice was much too big to blend with the bass section, and he did not read music that well. (Soloists rarely sing in a choir.) So when he made a mistake, which was often, it was deafening. Larisa the Red accompanied at the piano. I was happy to see Larisa the Blonde in the soprano section and Sergei translating as usual. Our first rehearsal was a joyful reunion, and the new members soon felt part of the family. The Americans mixed well with the Ukrainians and formed friendships.

Though the rehearsals were fun, life at home was difficult. Every night we were besieged with mosquitoes. They lived invisibly on the ceiling and attacked just after the lights went out, buzzing around our ears. They especially liked our hands, biting between the fingers. Every morning we had a new collection of bites. Finally I found some netting at the hardware store. The only color available was bright orange. I nailed it to the window frames. It looked ugly, but it helped.

The laundry pile grew daily. With three teenage boys in the house and no washing machine, we had a crisis. I did laundry the Ukrainian way, washing clothes in the bathtub, stirring with the end of a broom handle. Then I carted the heavy, wet clothes to the balcony, and hung them on the clotheslines. When they were dry, they were still not clean, having absorbed the dirty smell of the air around them. I was about to lose my sanity when I found a government laundry that would do shirts, socks, and underwear. (Other laundries had told me they laundered only sheets and towels.) It was expensive—two dollars for twenty pounds—and it was five miles from home. Because we had no car, we took suitcases full of laundry on the tram, the bus, and by foot one hour each way. But, oh, the joy of clean socks and sweet-smelling shirts and blouses! I was in heaven!

The five of us lived in close quarters with one bathroom, yet I reminded myself that this is typical of Ukrainian families. Three generations sometimes live in two rooms, sometimes with a dog as well. Even after we unpacked the boxes, it was hard to walk through the apartment with all the suitcases and piles of things that needed a shelf or a cupboard.

Our food supply traveled "from hand to mouth." Hands bought it in the morning and teenage mouths finished it by night. Though they hated peeling potatoes, the teenagers were good about going shopping. The bread store was a twenty-minute walk one way. The other stores were about the same, but in different directions. The boys especially liked to buy ice cream cones and strawberry soda. The sodas were heavy when loading thirteen bottles into a backpack. Consuming two sodas apiece, the group was often without anything to drink. Our water distiller could not compete with the thirst of nine people on a hot summer day. It took eight hours to make one gallon of distilled water. We sometimes resorted to hot tea with boiled tap water. The ice cream cones were also purchased in quantity, stored unwrapped in the small freezer of my 1950-style refrigerator, which often needed defrosting.

During the day, our apartment was the group activity center: peeling potatoes, organizing choir folders, and collating music. Everyone had a task. Dwight could not carry heavy groceries or walk very far, but he organized the music folders daily. When that was finished, I asked him to create an escape ladder of some nylon rope, and he sat on the balcony tying knots, worrying about our safety. We were on the fifth floor and had one exit to the stairwell. There were double doors at that exit, the inner wooden door with three locks and the outer steel door that also locked. Because Americans were advised to have steel doors for security, George had installed it last year. We left it unlocked at night in case of fire and the need for a quick escape.

Maynard Sikes, an engineer who helped to develop the Patriot Missile, was handy with repairs and fixed door locks, leaky faucets, and crooked cupboard doors. He was amazed and frustrated that most things in the apartment were not square. The floors sloped down toward the center of the room. The corners never met properly. It was as if the rooms had been constructed by children. Nancy, his wife, was usually in the kitchen, helping with preparation and cleanup, the jobs nobody liked.

The main meal of the day was late night supper after rehearsal. The nine of us usually sat down at the extended table at 11:00 P.M. We learned to alter the menu of "beef roast, potatoes, and carrots cooked in a large pot" with "pork roast, potatoes, and carrots cooked in a large pot." It was never a surprise, but there was always enough.

During the day, the balcony had a pleasant view. The tall trees blowing in the gentle breeze partially concealed the ugliness of the neighboring Soviet apartment buildings. In the distance across the gravel soccer field was School #191 where George McCammon held worship services. On Sunday mornings we gathered there with the parishioners of the Church of St. Andrew. Music Helen, our nickname for this attractive brunette with a gentle manner, directed the choir, a group of fourteen professional singers who were paid one dollar a week. There are no volunteer choirs in Ukraine. The service was in Ukrainian and English. George preached in English with Sergei Basarab as his translator.

Anna was no longer conducting the children's choir, nor was Larisa playing piano, but the new director and accompanist were very good. I was pleased to hear the children singing several of the songs I had taught them. Bogdana and Aksana were so glad to see me. We often sat together in church. I could tell that they were growing in their faith.

When the youth pastor left the church, Matthew McMurrin and Matthew McCammon became co-leaders of the teenage Bible class. From this beginning Matthew McMurrin began his own ministry with youth, leading Bible studies and starting a basketball ministry with the guys of the neighborhood. He would teach them American basketball and then invite them to study the Bible with him. The group grew through the winter until he had forty young men coming to basketball practice. Then they closed the school gymnasium for renovation. He was able to personally witness to others as his skill in speaking Russian grew rapidly, however.

George was busy opening his new school, St. Andrew's Preparatory School, where Roger and I would teach and Matthew would

be a student. There were shipments of supplies for the school to be
unloaded and painting to be done. The teenagers helped to prepare the school when they weren't shopping for food or singing at
rehearsals.

It was a busy two-and-one-half weeks. We had no time to worry
about the future—just take care of the present. Not only were we
working in the apartment and helping at the school, but in our
many rehearsals we also had prepared fifteen selections of music,
most of them American spirituals, and all in English.

The concert, entitled "Spirituals Plus" was held at the Lenin
Museum. The new government had changed the museum's name
to the Ukrainian House of Culture, and Lenin's statue had been
removed. Strange Soviet customs remained, however. There were
six doors across the front of the building followed by another set
of six doors inside. The audience was forced to enter the far left
door (the others were locked) and then proceed through the far
right door to enter the lobby. After the concert began, all the doors
were locked and tied with chains. What a disaster if there had
been a fire!

All the texts of the American spirituals were printed in the
Ukrainian language so that the audience could understand the
songs, most of which were a cappella. Roger spoke to the audience between numbers with Sergei at his side. He talked about
the history of the spiritual, the sadness of slavery, and the promise of heaven for the believer. The oval theater provided a more
intimate atmosphere than the cathedral of last summer.

The Ukrainians identified with the spirituals. They had been
slaves of Communism. The choir loved the rhythm and spirit of
this music, and their faces glowed as they performed the concert.
The audience loved it too and applauded profusely. Our American
singers were thrilled about the performance. Afterwards, we walked
across the street to the Dnieper Hotel restaurant to celebrate their

last night in Kiev. Dwight paid the bill for dinner for eleven people, totaling twenty-one dollars.

Five days earlier Roger had celebrated another birthday at rehearsal. The choir brought flowers and sang songs of congratulations. Seeing their outpouring of love and now knowing many choir members himself, Blair, one of our American teenagers, said to Roger, "I thought you were crazy to move here, but now I understand. It's the people!"

Chapter 11

On Our Own

The day after the spirituals concert our American friends left Kiev. As we bid goodbye at the railroad station, and they boarded the same car #5 to Budapest, I was bracing myself for the time to come—living in Kiev as a family of three instead of nine. They seemed to be more worried about us than we were. The adults were tearful as they said goodbye.

"Are you going to be OK?" Nancy asked, giving me a worried look, as if she expected me to say "no." Maynard had made a tape of our concert on his digital recorder, and he was playing the music as the train pulled away from the station. Soon they were out of sight.

"Well, it's just us now," Roger said as he put his arm on Matthew's shoulder. It was dawning upon us that we were here for more than a holiday.

By the time we got home, we had plenty to think about. We were told that our landlord might refuse to sign the lease because he wanted his apartment back. After three weeks, we were certainly not ready to move. Our eighty dollars a month rent was all we could afford, and I was distressed to think of being homeless in Ukraine—already!

Toni McCammon cheered me up by suggesting we go to a Ukrainian beauty salon. Her translator, Humanitarian Helen, whose nickname reflected her job with humanitarian aid, made an appointment for us for the next day. I had not had a perm since mid-April, no color or cut since mid-June. My hair was straight and unkempt. What I needed first was a cut and permanent. Toni had recommended the large salon in the center of town. We met outside of the building which had attractive pictures of various hairstyles on the windows. Toni had brought Helen along to translate. The three of us had not had lunch, so we purchased ice cream bars on the street. *I hope they don't mind us bringing food inside,* I thought.

We entered the door into a dingy hallway leading past a long room full of hairdressers each at a small, crowded station. Helen led us to the second floor. *Aha! That must have been the training school, and here are the real hairdressers,* I thought. The whole building looked like a prison—cement walls in dark green and brown. In the upstairs hall were six chairs, filled with people waiting, forlorn expressions on their faces. We walked right past them into the salon room.

Before me was a young woman about thirty years old, with light blond hair, attractively styled except for the tinge of pink on the back of her head. She spoke no English. Helen told her who I was and reminded her of our appointment. She motioned for me to sit down in her chair, and I did. She looked at my hair, fingering its various lengths, and told me to go back downstairs and get it washed but not to dry it. Then she handed me a plastic bottle with pink liquid in it and a small dish towel.

I walked out into the hall and down the stairs with Helen to another dreary room with a long, low sink against one wall. It looked like a trough with six sets of faucets and sprayers attached. Ladies were leaning over and washing their own hair. I approached the trough and bent over. The collar of my blouse fell forward into my face, getting wet with the hose. It was a trick handling the sprayer, the two faucets, and the bottle of shampoo. There was no shelf so the plastic bottle kept falling over in the bottom of the trough, thereby getting even more watered-down with the water from everyone else's head. Finally, feeling very awkward, I wrapped my hair into the tiny towel and composed myself to go upstairs for my "perm."

When I sat back into the chair, the hairdresser named Larisa dropped a basket of permanent rollers into my lap and indicated that I should hand them individually to her. Then she pulled my head back so that I could not see the basket. As I lifted them out, I saw they were made of gray wood with a thick, black rubber band coming out of one end, made to attach to the carved grooves on the other end.

"I want a gentle curl," I told Helen. "Is there a larger size?" There were no other sizes. But some of the wooden rollers were a little bit larger than the others. Toni and Helen went through the basket to see if they could pick out the ones that might be slightly larger. They handed them to me, and I handed them to Larisa. I felt like Wilma Flintstone in Bedrock having her hair done with cat bones. Besides that, Larisa was sponging my hair in large sections from a bowl of some chemical solution before she put the rollers in. There were no permanent wave papers used and no squeeze bottle.

After the curlers were in place, she just dabbed my curlered head with the same sponge and then covered it with a plastic bag. She held up eight fingers, saying, "Eight minutes under the dryer."

I walked down the same dreary hallway and stairs to an alcove covering twelve metal dryers from the 1940s. Each one had two switches on the front of the hood: Off/On and High/Low heat. I sat under the dryer thinking, *What have I done? What have I done?*

Meanwhile Larisa was cutting Toni's hair short, and I mean *short!* It was tapered so close to the back of her neck, it seemed shaved. But then Toni looks good in anything.

After eight minutes, I went upstairs. Larisa took off the plastic, inspected my curl, and said with fingers spread, "Ten more minutes."

Toni was finished, and Helen said it was time for her to leave, too. I was going to have to finish this alone. What would happen to my hair if I sat under a dryer for ten minutes with these strange chemicals?

It was too late to turn back. *At least I won't put it on high heat,* I thought. Ten minutes later, I was inspected again. "Five more minutes," Larisa said. Oh dear! Why hadn't I gone to the Dnieper Hotel and spent $60 instead of $6? It's my head, for goodness sake!

Finally, after five minutes, Larisa said, *"Harasha!"* (Good!) She led me back down to the shampoo room and pointed me to Maria, a homely little woman who swept the floors. "Five minutes, then ten minutes," she said with appropriate finger motions. Then she left us.

Maria gave me another tiny towel, and led me to the trough. I bent over, and she sprayed hot, and I mean *hot,* water on my head for five minutes with one hand while she slapped my curlered head with the other. *I can't believe this,* I thought. *I am an idiot!*

Then she wrapped my head in the towel and led me to the center of the room to a black vinyl chair that had holes in it. The stuffing was spilling out. There was a bowl of liquid beside it on a small table. A sponge was floating in the liquid. Thankful I had not worn a silk blouse, I cringed, wondering what the next step would be. Sure enough, I got "sponged" again. Then she moved my hand up, to hold the towel around my curlers. There I sat, like a statue in this ridiculous position.

As she sat there next to me, neither of us said a word. Embarrassed at the silence, I tried some Russian words I had been learning. "Ten minutes," I said, showing her I understood. "Yes," she said, showing that she understood me. That was the end of that conversation.

Two long minutes later I asked, "What is your name?" "Maria," she replied. "My name is Diane," I said. She nodded. Well, that was the end of *that* conversation. Every minute of silence was an uncomfortable eternity.

After eight minutes had passed, I did say something about Florida, and she said, "New York" mixed with other things I did not understand. That lasted about five seconds. Finally it was time to move.

She rinsed my curlers at the trough, then took me to the black chair and proceeded to remove them, showing me to hold my hands like a bird's nest so she could drape my towel over my hands and have a basket to hold the curlers. There was no mirror in the room to see what I looked like. Finally she put a towel on my head, and I put the curlers next to the bowl on the table and went upstairs.

As I sat again in Larisa's chair, I saw myself in the mirror. *Not too bad,* I thought, raising my eyebrows. I couldn't tell the condition of my hair, but the curl looked good—not tight, not stringy. Larisa asked me in body language where the permanent curlers were. I pointed that I had left them downstairs. Larisa shrugged as if to say, "Don't you know how to do anything right?"

She began to cut my hair, taking off a half inch in large sections, not the precision cutting the way that American hairdressers do. Then Larisa took a key from her drawer and went to a locked cabinet to get the setting rollers. She brought back a plastic bag filled with rollers of different colors, sizes, and styles—most of them with brushes inside. She washed the combs in a small sink before she set my hair. I handed her the brush rollers—after picking out large clumps of black hair from the brushes—and she fastened them in my hair with large, black bobby pins. Once my hair was set, she held up her ten fingers three times and said something that meant "Thirty minutes."

I went downstairs again. This time I alternated between the high and low heat settings. I was really anxious to get out of there as soon as possible. Next reading: "Ten more minutes." Finally the rollers were taken out. A yellow organza cape was placed around my shoulders, and Larisa began combing my hair, teasing it and playing with it.

Some of her friends came in, and they were laughing and talking. Larisa laughed, too, stopped combing my hair, looked at herself in the mirror, and started restyling her hair with the same comb. Then she went back to combing my hair again. The style was finessed and ready for a light touch of hair spray. She took out a brown squeeze bottle and squirted a film of something that smelled like furniture polish.

That night at rehearsal, many people said that my hair looked absolutely perfect. I knew it needed some hair color now, but I waited three weeks. I was in shock over the whole salon experience, and I wanted to give my hair enough time to recover too.

The same day that I visited the hair salon, Roger opened a bank account. Few people used banks in Ukraine. They thought their money was safer hidden at home. Roger was hoping that

businesses in Ukraine would place paid advertising in our concert programs or become sponsors. To receive money for advertising, he needed a bank account. He went to the Aggio Bank to
deposit $150 American dollars and some coupons (the Ukrai-
nian currency) with Translator Helen.

Translator Helen is not the same person as Humanitarian Helen
or Music Helen. Since last names were so hard to remember, we
followed George McCammon's tradition of referring to our Ukrainians by their first name and what they did. Humanitarian Helen
ran the humanitarian aid ministry for George; Music Helen directed the music at his church; and Translator Helen assisted Roger
at business meetings. There was also Computer Yuri, Banker Yuri,
Preacher Sasha, etc.

Climbing a shabby staircase, Roger and Helen found the bank
on the third floor. *They certainly don't waste their investments on
property improvement,* he thought. After passing through several
checkpoints, they entered a room where three bank officers were
sitting at individual desks with computers, none of which were
being used. Roger talked to the man at the far end of the room for
almost an hour, discussing procedures and services of the bank.
He learned that if he opened a coupon account, he would receive a
50 percent annual interest rate. That sounds good. However, the
coupon had lost 60 percent of its value during the past three weeks
due to inflation. Not so good! In July 1992, a dollar had been worth
165 coupons. In July 1993, a dollar was 4,500, and now one month
later it was 8,500.

Also if coupons are transferred from another source into his
account, there is a 16 percent service charge. If the transfer is more
than 20,000,000 coupons (equal that day to $2,353), the rate goes
up to 20 percent.

Having learned the frightening news about the coupon account, Roger asked him about opening a dollar account. The man
said that for hard currency there was only a 2 percent fee for a
transfer. No interest was paid on the account, however. When
you withdraw all the money, the bank keeps the last fifty dollars.
There are no checks in Kiev. All transactions are in cash. Finally

he was told if he wanted to change coupons into dollars at the bank, he would have to pay twice the exchange rate, paying 17,000 coupons to buy one dollar, instead of the 8,500 rate on the street.

During this long conversation, the other two bank officers watched the men talk. They had nothing else to do.

Roger decided to set up two accounts—one for dollars and one for coupons. After filling out the papers, he went to another room where a lady gave him a computer form. "Fill out this form and take it to Mr. Boiko in Room 312," she said. Finding Mr. Boiko, Roger offered him all the papers he had filled out plus the $150. "Go away!" he said, "I'm on break! Come back tomorrow!"

There were twelve other employees in this room. Helen bravely went to an imposing man in the back of the room for some assistance. For two or three minutes, they yelled at each other. Finally, the man pointed to the clerk at the other end of the room. With Helen by his side, Roger brought the $150 and the papers to the clerk. She quickly sifted through the small pile of bills and came to a $100 bill that had been folded twice, heavily creased. She threw the bill on the table. "This isn't any good," she said. "You must get me other money."

Roger had lost his patience. "This is perfectly good money," he said hotly, but she would not take it. "*We* are leaving!" said Roger as he scooped up everything from the table.

Roger and Helen left the room and went down the stairs. There they ran into the first bank officer. Helen told the man of their dilemma. Apologetic, the officer immediately led them to the vice president's office, elaborately furnished, and he listened to Roger's story. Now relaxed, Roger joked that there must be a purpose that they should meet. Perhaps his bank would like to become a sponsor of Roger's concerts. They exchanged business cards; the vice president gave directives to his assistants; and Roger soon had his new bank accounts.

As Roger left the building, he said to Helen, "If it takes three hours to put money *into* the bank, how long will it take to get the money *out?*"

Chapter 12
Living in the Neighborhood

As the first of September approached, we were walking through the initial adjustments to a foreign culture. Our nine-story apartment building was like a long ship with fourteen entrances on one side. Over two thousand people lived there, and the narrow street that connected the entrances was very dark at night. Other buildings like ours surrounded School #191 and the gravel sports yard where the children played. There were shops, a post office, and other schools twenty minutes away. Our region Bereznikee was one of the fourteen regions of Kiev, each with an average population of 200,000 people. With an additional 500,000 people living outside the city limits, the total population was 3,300,000 people. Within each region were micro-regions with their own schools, bread store, post office, and a few gastronomes (government food stores).

Our local neighborhood was a walking city. The fifteen-minute walk to the nearest bus stop meant traveling broken sidewalks or dirt paths. Even in the dark of night, people were walking everywhere. There were places where pipes crossed over the sidewalks, so it was important to memorize those points when you were walking in the dark. These pipes connected the watering system for the yards. Two-foot-high fences made out of green painted pipes squirt water from the tiny drilled holes. The water helped the weeds to grow higher, for the grass was never cut during the summer.

Bogdana and Oksana became my young companions. They helped me shop for food. Walking for an hour around the neighborhood, I could visit the bread store and two gastronomes that sold sugar, butter, soft drinks, and rice. The other items I could get at the open-air market, twenty minutes away by bus. This was the same market we had visited last summer. As time went by, I realized that this free-enterprise system was indirectly supervised through the Mafia.

It was important to remember to bring your own container for every purchase, for bags were not provided. The bread came unwrapped, passed hand to hand at the bread store. If you wanted to buy sour cream at the gastronome, you must bring a jar and hopefully a plastic cap. Milk came to the neighborhood in a tank on the back of a truck. Bring a bucket and wait in line for the hose and the attendant who served you. Woe to the person who forgot to boil the milk!

Bogdana and Oksana taught me necessary Russian words in order to shop. Though the Ukrainian language was beginning its revival at that time, most people still spoke Russian. *"Skolka?"* meant "How much?" The answer was given in numbers as cost per kilogram. If I couldn't understand the number, I sheepishly handed the seller a piece of paper and a pencil to write it for me. The girls giggled at my pronunciations, but through trial and error, I improved.

Matthew was a willing helper in gathering food, probably because he ate more food than both his parents. He was learning Russian faster than I, so he was more confident to explore new territory. One day Matthew and I rode the bus to another section of town, to a government supermarket that had grocery carts. They were small and resembled recycled wire, but it was an unexpected convenience. We gathered three loaves of bread, a bag of cookies, thirty eggs in my egg carrier (a square, molded plastic container with handles), and thirty glass bottles of Pepsi. "Are you sure you can carry thirty bottles?" I asked Matthew.

"No problem!" said Matt. "I've done it before. Thirty exactly fills this large backpack."

At the checkout counter, I put the bread and cookies in the plastic bag I had brought. Matthew packed the bottles of Pepsi in his gray canvas backpack.

Above the supermarket was a hardware store. "Let's go upstairs and see what they have," I said. By the time we reached the top of the stairs, Matthew said, "Mom, I think one of these drinks is leaking."

He unpacked some of the bottles onto the cement floor and discovered that one of them was indeed leaking. A mother with her little girl was standing nearby. Matthew took the partially open Pepsi to them and offered it to the little girl. The little girl looked surprised; the mother, suspicious. Yet they accepted it.

"Why don't you take my egg carrier and go on home," I said to Matt as we waited at the bus stop. "I think I'll go across the street and pick up some meat and vegetables at that open-air market." Matthew agreed and climbed onto the bus with his heavy backpack, carrying the egg carrier in one hand.

As the bus bounced its way down the road, Matthew noticed a small puddle forming under his feet. From the backpack came a small hissing sound. An elderly woman came up to him and motioned that his backpack was a nuisance, and he should take it off. As he put the backpack onto the floor of the bus, he noticed that the backs of his legs were sticky. It was impossible to unpack his cargo on the bouncing floor. He was unable to sit down because all the seats were full. Gingerly he held the eggs in his left hand while touching the top of the backpack with his right. A thin ribbon of liquid was running down the center of the floor. When the bus arrived twenty minutes later, he disembarked, placing the heavy backpack on his shoulders again. Walking the distance to the apartment building, he could feel the liquid oozing down his legs into his socks. Riding the elevator to the fifth floor, he watched his puddle grow.

Now he was finally at the door of the apartment. Holding the egg carrier in his left hand, he reached into his pocket for his keys. While he was attempting to unlock the steel door, the mace that was attached to his key ring flipped open its safety guard. Turning his face away, he tried to reattach the safety guard with his free hand. Pssst!

The red pepper gas spewed out. His lungs hurt and, for a moment, he couldn't see. Finally he turned the key in the lock, opened the lock on the inside wooden door, and headed for the kitchen.

He placed the Pepsi's on the kitchen table, finding four of them mostly empty. The eggs he placed in the large windowsill. Once in the bathroom, he showered immediately and washed his face carefully with a cloth. As he was dressing, he heard a crash from the kitchen. A Pepsi bottle had fallen off the uneven edge of the table and there was broken glass and sticky liquid all over the floor. Matthew groaned in frustration. He mopped up the mess with a cloth. When I returned with two beef roasts, green peppers, and some fruit, he greeted me with his tale of woe. "Why is everything so difficult here?" he said.

Actually Matthew could have been grateful that he had hot water for his shower. Such was not always the case. The hot water for the neighborhood came from one source. Some mornings before school, he turned on the water faucet only to get a groan from the pipes, no hot water at all. It was impossible to calculate the hours the hot water was running. Sometimes just after dinner, it would stop, which gave me a good excuse to postpone washing the dishes. If we were really desperate, we could heat water on the stove and pour it into a small amount of water in the bathtub. Toni said sometimes their building didn't have any water—hot or cold—and the residents had to get buckets of water from the lake to flush the toilets.

We shared our apartment with a large number of brown roaches. At first they were only in the kitchen and appeared at night from underneath the wallpaper. I kept the food sealed but shuddered to think of them crawling on my silverware and plates. In a few weeks, they were on my hands when I woke in the morning, and some found a home in our fax machine. I found their crushed bodies on my incoming faxes. I used the traditional methods of roach motels and such. Nothing worked. Finally George's missionary friend, Steve Luxemborg, came with his special spray. Though unavailable in America, it could be used in Africa. He covered his face with a towel and began spraying my empty cupboards. "Oh, my!" I heard him yell from the kitchen. "Roger, come here, quick!"

Steve and Roger started pulling off the wallpaper to reveal thousands of roaches. I hid in the other room with eyes closed, dreading what I knew they saw. Finally most of the battle was won. "I guess we will need some new wallpaper," Roger said as he came in the room, brushing his fingers through his hair to remove any remaining dead or dying creatures. I waited an hour before I ventured into the kitchen to sweep up the piles of dead bugs on the floor.

Whenever we left the apartment, we traveled in the small elevator just outside our steel door. The Satan worshiper who lived on the second floor had taken a knife to write in English in the wall, "I love death." He watched us come and go from his window, sometimes calling "Kill Florida" with loud heavy metal music blaring in the background. His straight, shoulder-length blond hair was an unusual appearance compared to other young Ukrainian men his age.

Matthew McCammon had drawn a cross inside the elevator door and written the words "Jesus loves you" in indelible marker encircled by a heart. No matter how hard the blond rebel tried, he could not remove those words or the cross.

One of our son Matthew's first Ukrainian friends was a young man we called Preacher Sasha. This athletic, twenty-three-year-old man was tall with dark hair, bright blue eyes, and a ruddy complexion. Though he had been a Christian for only six months, he was pastoring a young church in a neighboring region.

Sasha had met his first Christian when he was serving in the Russian army in northern Siberia. The older soldiers were cruel to the young newcomers and sometimes would beat them. They often wanted Sasha to fight them, because he was a kickboxer. Sasha was afraid of their mean treatment, yet he noticed one man in the company who was never afraid, nor was he harmed.

"Why is it that you are so brave?" Sasha had asked him.

"I'm a Christian," replied the believer. "I have Jesus." This young man showed Sasha a Bible—the first Bible Sasha had ever seen. He talked with Sasha about his faith, and Sasha found his ideas interesting. A few years later, while working as a guard at a kindergarten, Sasha met a little American girl named Sara. Since he knew some English, Sasha helped her communicate with the other children. Her father was an American missionary working with George McCammon's church, and Sasha joined his Bible class. It wasn't long until Sasha accepted Christ and began to work in George's ministry. One of the top students at his university, Sasha quickly became a scholar of this Bible that was so new to him. A few months later, when a church group from America came to town, Sasha was chosen as the Ukrainian they wanted to be pastor of the little church they had planted. Though his last name was Sikorsky, the name Preacher Sasha seemed to fit this extraordinary young man.

Sasha Sikorsky heard Matthew playing the piano at George's home. "I have a piano, but I have never learned to play," said Sasha. "I think I will give it to you. You need to have a piano in your home."

We were amazed at his generosity. Sasha had very few belongings: some books, and a cassette tape player. He lived in a two-room apartment with his mother and had rented out his room to a Japanese student. He wanted so much to learn the Japanese language. Every night he slept on a vinyl lawn chair in his mother's room.

Arrangements were made to move the piano from the fourth floor of Sasha's building to the fifth floor of ours. We rented a truck, and Stanislav volunteered to help. Stanislav was incredibly strong and bullheaded. He could lift one end of the upright piano with four men lifting the other. Carrying the piano down four flights of stairs, they loaded it onto the truck and brought it to our building.

The tiny elevator was just big enough for the piano, if standing vertically on its end. Stanislav was ready to push it in without any protection. "Wait!" cried Roger. "Wrap it with this cardboard first." Stanislav was not planning to wait. He wanted to shove it in and get it finished. Roger stood eyeball to eyeball with the big man. Finally, Stanislav allowed Roger to wrap the piano first. There was only one scratch on the shiny veneer surface when it arrived at our apartment.

Step by step the apartment was becoming more organized. George's lease on the flat ended on September 1, and we did not know if the owner would rent to us or take it back. On August 25, the landlord announced we could rent it for six months to a year for $85 a month. We were so relieved. We immediately made plans to have the dirty, unfinished wooden floors sanded and lacquered. Eugenia, a choir member and businesswoman, recommended a man named Ivan who had done work for her company.

The next day Eugenia arrived in a company car with Ivan, who unloaded a large sanding machine, the size of a wheelbarrow, from the trunk. To prepare for them, we had moved all the furniture from the two larger rooms into the hall, the balcony, and the small room, which had now become Matthew's bedroom. We swept the floors of the empty rooms thoroughly, but the dirt kept appearing. "Where does this dirt come from?" I asked, in exasperation. Yet I was so excited to finally see some progress toward the remodeling of this dirty apartment.

But my expectations were soon deflated. There would be no work today. The supervisor of the building had to give permission to allow the machine to be plugged into the special outlet for remodeling work in the stairwell. Perhaps tomorrow!

The next morning at 7:30, the sanding process began. The machine revealed beautiful wood underneath the years of dirt and stain. Ivan worked with great care, sanding by hand the perimeter of each room. By afternoon he had finished. He swept the floor free of dust and was ready for the first coat of varnish.

"Where is the varnish?" he asked me through Bogdana.

"What do you mean?" I replied.

Bogdana explained, "When you hire a workman to repair your apartment, you must provide all the supplies: hammers for carpenters, paint and brushes for painters, and lacquer for floor work."

We searched all the hardware stores that we knew. None of them had any lacquer. The work had come to a standstill. We alerted the choir that we needed fourteen quarts of floor lacquer. Surely somewhere in a city where there are millions of apartments, there had to be some of this stuff.

Giving up the project for the day, I went to St. Andrew's Preparatory School where I taught every day from twelve until two. It was a seventeen-minute walk from home. I supervised four teenagers in their individual English courses. I enjoyed helping the students. Also this daily routine of responsibility added order to my life. No matter how dreary I felt when I was walking to school, I had a spring in my step coming home.

Stopping at the bread store after school was a good idea, since it was in my path. Yet it was always closed from two to three o'clock, as were all the stores, when the employees had their break. So I would often visit for an extra hour in the office with Humanitarian Helen or Mr. Hjelmfeld, who was also an American volunteer teacher. David Hjelmfeld taught economics and helped in administration. His wife, Kendall, taught fourth through sixth grades. I was complaining to them about the absence of floor lacquer in the city. Mr. Hjelmfeld said that if we ever found it, we could stay at their apartment while the lacquer dried. They had an extra room not far from the school.

Days later a choir member arrived at our apartment with the necessary *lac*, which was the Russian word for lacquer. We moved our things to the Hjelmfelds' apartment while Matt moved in with Matthew McCammon. We had been told, "Three coats of lacquer, three days. Then move all the furniture into the two finished rooms and three more days for lacquering the other half of the apartment."

The six days turned into two weeks because the weather became damp and rainy. I tried to stay in the apartment to work on my computer while Ivan worked, but the fumes from the lacquer burned my lungs. How could Ivan stand it? He didn't even wear a mask.

Every day after school I walked to the apartment to test the floor. Still sticky! The deluge of rain was keeping it from drying. Finally the day arrived when the first half of the apartment was dry. We could not move all the furniture to the other two rooms without help. Roger was rehearsing the choir that night and said he would ask for volunteers from the choir, whose number had grown from fifty to eighty.

As I was sitting at the Hjelmfelds' apartment that evening, studying Russian, I said to Kendall, "It is such a miserable, wet night that I know Roger won't get any volunteers, not on such short notice."

At that moment, David Hjelmfeld returned home from a Bible study at George's church. "Tonight the teacher asked, 'If you had all the money in the world, what would you buy?'" David told us, "I was thinking to myself: a condo, a golf course . . . and then one of the Ukrainian men spoke up, saying, 'I'd buy a pair of shoes.'"

As we were reflecting on this sad comment, the telephone rang. It was Roger. Four friends were coming with Matthew to help us move the furniture. In fact they had already left. Would I please hurry over and unlock the apartment and supervise until Roger got there?

I grumbled to myself all the way, walking in the cold, dark rain for twenty minutes. I was grateful for the help, but I would have preferred another time. When I arrived, Matthew and the others were already there, and things were in mass chaos. "Where do you want this? Where do you want that? What's next?" There were a thousand items to move, most of them small. Soon I was dumping everything into boxes and drawers and throwing them into corners, working as fast as I could. When Roger arrived, he started giving contrary orders, which complicated the process even more, but soon we were finished.

Then Roger insisted on serving everyone tea, and of course, there was no place to sit down. We had the piano in the kitchen, and we were running into each other. But we survived the confusion and were left with a sink full of dirty dishes.

By now it was almost midnight, and we had to return to the other apartments to sleep. Roger and I were standing with Matthew in the rain at the bus stop. The bus would stop first at the Hjelmfelds' building and then continue to the McCammons' where Matt was staying. We waited in the wind and pelting rain for twenty minutes. No bus. The back of my neck and hair were cold and wet. So were my feet. We turned and walked down an alley, which was a shorter way to walk to the McCammons' home. We did not want Matthew to walk alone at this late hour.

Forty yards into the alley, we heard the bus. Rats! It was too late to run and catch it. Roger gave me his backpack of music and the umbrella, and told me to walk to the Hjelmfelds. He would walk Matthew home.

We parted and walked our separate dark paths. I was aware of something following me. I turned to see a large German shepherd at my heels. "Go away," I said to him firmly, but then I saw how miserable he was too, like me, in the rain and the cold. Usually I would be nervous about these wild dogs, who roamed the neighborhoods fighting with each other and threatening those who approached their domain. But I was too numb and too tired to care. We walked for a time together, and then he sauntered off toward another building. I ended my journey in ankle deep water as I approached the Hjelmfelds' building. *I can't wait to get under my warm, blue blanket,* I thought.

I walked into the stairwell, which was lit by one lightbulb on the grayish-blue cement wall. The Hjelmfelds had two doors. The first door unlocked to a small hall with three apartments. The center one was theirs. So there were two doors to unlock and two keys. It was 12:45 A.M., and Roger had forgotten to give me the keys. I just couldn't ring the doorbell and wake them in the middle of the night. I would wait until Roger came back from the McCammons.

Thirty minutes later Roger arrived, surprised to see me standing in the dim stairwell. He sheepishly apologized. When we entered the apartment, Kendall was still grading her school papers. I had stood in the cold, damp hall unnecessarily. It was one of my many lessons in learning patience.

Chapter 13
A Spiritual Message

Roger chose to repeat the performance of the *Messiah* at the Dome Organi Musiki (House of Organ Music) as the next concert. The news that this American had returned to live in Kiev interested many people.

At Radio Station #1, Roger was interviewed about his life. The host, who had a picture of Jesus on his desk, asked Roger, "What is your spiritual purpose for being here?" followed by the question, "Is this why you have chosen to do Handel's *Messiah*?" Roger was amazed by these questions. Was the man really asking them, or was an angel speaking the words in his mouth to broadcast such thoughts over government radio? Roger seized the opportunity to share his heart with the people.

Roger was also hoping to perform the Brahms *Requiem* at the Opera House the following month. He met with the director of the Opera Theater to discuss his plans. Mr. Chuprina asked him, "In the program you are presenting, will there be anything of spiritual content?"

Roger, not wanting to offend this man on their first meeting, spoke guardedly, "This is a musical concert, not a religious service."

"Yes," said Mr. Chuprina, "but will you talk about a spiritual message?"

Roger hedged again, "Well, you know that Brahms wrote this for all of the German people . . . "

Mr. Chuprina stood up and leaned over the desk, looking into Roger's eyes. "I'm *asking* you if you have a spiritual message. Our people *need* a spiritual message!" he said emphatically.

It became clear that, as a musician, Roger had a unique opportunity. The arts represented the soul of the Ukrainian people. Their poets, composers, and artists were highly regarded. If we could bring the spiritual message through music, their longing hearts would hear and be touched. However, not everyone who mentioned the word "spiritual" was defining a religious need. Rather they were looking toward a satisfaction of the soul. We knew that the answer was Jesus Christ.

Our new direction must be the establishment of a concert series in Kiev. Roger designed an ambitious schedule—six concerts in four months. He printed a brochure announcing the names and dates of the concerts, to be distributed at the first performance of *Messiah*.

When he showed the brochure to George McCammon, George scolded him, "Roger, what you are attempting is impossible! How do you expect to teach at the school and have enough time left to execute all these concerts? Living in Ukraine is difficult at a slow pace, let alone this craziness. Your marriage will suffer because of it. And how do you expect to afford it?"

"I'll live by faith," answered Roger. Nothing George could say deterred him from his goal. "Conducting is my gift, and I *have* to do this."

Though we were responsible for raising our own money, George was technically our boss. We accepted our donations through his organization called Lifeline Ministries. August contributions had been low—only $500—but because our living expenses were so low, we still had some money to invest in another concert. In the first "Spirituals Plus" concert, the rehearsal and concert halls had been free, and the choir had cost $11 per person for two and a half weeks' work. How would we continue?

Would September contributions be better? The *Messiah* concert would require an orchestra—an extra $600—and we would need to rent the Dome Organi Musiki. There would also be publicity costs. If we paid these expenses for the *Messiah* concert, we would have nothing left for rent or food. We would have to trust the Lord to provide from the September contributions. Roger told me that he knew the Lord wanted this concert, and I believed him.

I started writing a general letter to those who had given us farewell financial donations as well as our eleven pledged supporters. "They must know what is going on here," I said to Roger. I faxed the letter to my friend Nancy Lindborg in Orlando, Florida, and she had it duplicated and mailed to thirty-seven friends. We called it "Notes from the McMurrins."

The day of the *Messiah* concert was very cold. I stayed inside the Hjelmfelds' apartment, counting out dollars in small denominations. I inserted $1,100 into 105 envelopes for three weeks of rehearsal pay for the choir plus $600 for the orchestra. Then I stuffed the envelopes into Zip-Lock plastic bags and placing them in a large purse, I headed for the bus stop. In less than an hour, Roger was expecting me at the Dome Organi Musiki. The rain had stopped, but the temperature was much colder.

Worried about my carrying so much cash, David and Kendall Hjelmfeld came with me. I wore a purple wool suit and a white rabbit jacket. It was the warmest thing I owned. I had planned to buy a winter coat in December when I would return to the States, and this cold weather was unexpected for a Floridian. As I climbed into the long yellow bus, I felt conspicuous among the drably dressed people of the neighborhood—like a snow bunny in the Black Forest. *It's all right, I told myself. Roger will be dressed in tails, and I will look out of place either here or there.*

We arrived at the metro station and climbed the dirty gray steps to the platform. Seeing the train had just arrived, I ran forward to the door, not knowing that the Hjelmfelds were some distance behind me. I tried to hold the doors open. But they forcibly closed on my arm, clasping it like a vice. No one inside the car offered to help me. Mr. Hjelmfeld ran forward, and we pulled and pulled until my arm slid free. Moments later the train raced away. So much for safety features! I was thankful that I was not pulled down the track: a piece of bunny fur with a person attached, flying through the air.

Arriving at the Dome Organi Musiki, we waited our turn to go through the tiny two-foot-wide door, the only door that was open to admit the audience.

Once inside, I wandered backstage looking for Roger. When did he want me to pay the orchestra? I knew I would pay the singers at the reception afterwards. Since Roger was not there, I headed toward the hall. The five-minute warning bell sounded, and Stanislav came through the door, almost knocking me down. He was the bass soloist and was not even dressed for the concert yet. He carried his tux on a hanger over his shoulder. I just shook my head, wondering how 160 Ukrainians would ever be ready for a concert on time. Several of them were still in the hall talking to friends. I took my seat, holding the money bag on my lap.

I noticed that the Ukrainian man beside me had no program. We had taken great pains to print a sixteen-page program containing the entire text of *Messiah* in the Ukrainian and English languages with an attractive four-color cover.

As I looked around, I saw that no one had a program. I jumped up with my purse on my arm and headed for the rear of the cathedral. There were the programs still wrapped in brown paper on the floor. Bogdana and Oksana were nearby.

"Here!" I said to them, "Help me pass out these programs. Quickly!"

I went down the center aisle passing the programs on each side. The girls remained at the door handing programs to the newcomers. The orchestra was taking their places, but I continued to walk the aisle, "*Programme*? Do you have a *programme*?" I kept asking. "No, they're free. Take one." Where were the ushers? They were being paid to do this! Now the latecomers thought I was the usher and asked me where their seats were. I helped as much as I could.

I returned to the rear of the hall for more programs. George McCammon was on the podium with Sergei, giving an introduction to the concert, followed by the opening prayer. Roger came onto the podium, looking dapper in his tails and white tie. Rats! I was stuck at the rear of the hall. The overture had already begun.

I sedately lifted the cord the usher had drawn across the center aisle and slowly started to make my way to my seat. Then I stopped in my tracks. Three television cameramen were blocking the center aisle about midway to the front. I could not go around them without ruining their shot. I returned to the back of the hall, squeezed myself through the standing-room-only crowd, and followed the row of massive pillars that supported the cathedral-like room, all the way to the front. How undignified I must have looked! I approached my seat on the last three measures of the overture and sat down on the cut-off with upturned face ready for the opening recitative, "Comfort ye!," trying not to breathe too loudly from the exertion of getting there.

The first half of the concert was splendid. The tempos were exciting, the soloists expressive, and the choir really knew the work and performed their English with near perfection. I lost my queasiness about the problems of the "house" in the thrill of the performance.

At intermission Roger was really upset about the programs and house management. He had paid extra to have it managed well. I tried to soothe him, but the only thing that worked was for me to say, "I'll take care of it." Then out I went into the crowd, passing out more programs, this time to the right and left transepts. The hall was packed. It was difficult to move through so many people.

After the performance Roger was surrounded by admirers. The director of the Conservatory was thrilled by the performance and invited Roger to his club, where the President of Ukraine visits. Two radio stations interviewed Roger about his music. They asked me questions about living in Ukraine.

Still carrying the $1,500 in my purse, I was anxious to pay the orchestra. When I presented the packet of envelopes to the orchestra's representative, the man wanted to argue the price with me. He did not want to accept the $15 per player, but insisted on $25.

He had previously agreed to $15, but Edward Senko, our manager, had not gotten it in writing. "I am not prepared to pay more than was originally agreed upon," I said. "You can have that amount now or renegotiate and be paid later. I don't make decisions. I am only the messenger." They decided to wait.

The chaos of the evening had been almost too much for me. I do not handle confrontation well. I could not get close to Roger for help on these matters, so I went to the reception at the music school next door to meet the choir members and pass out their envelopes. By delightful contrast, the singers were so happy. I knew all 105 of them by name by attending rehearsals and keeping the attendance records. They hugged me and said wonderful things. Roger received a great ovation when he entered the room. We were off to a fine start.

The director of the music school was at the party. "Please feel free to use my school anytime," she said. "I am a Christian. I know Jesus sent you." I gave her all the flowers that Roger received from the audience. When she protested, I insisted, "The flowers will not last on the long ride by metro and bus." Finally, she did accept them for the school.

Carrying a suitcase of orchestra music, Roger and I went home that night on public transportation. The bus arrived at the Hjelmfelds' apartment shortly after midnight. As we stepped down onto the street, Roger twisted his ankle in a nasty hole. He limped his way to the door, and we fell into bed, happy but exhausted.

We went to sleep with peaceful hearts, remembering a man's comment after the performance: "This concert has stirred my religious feelings. May I come to your church?"

God was working the splendor of His music in visible ways. Perhaps that was the message to us through the verse in Isaiah, "I have endowed you with splendor." The splendor was in the music. It was flowing through us by God's design. Despite the frustrations of the evening, His blessing brought satisfaction to our souls.

Chapter 14

Two Million Coupons
and Nothing to Buy

The next day our major business was to take two million coupons out of the bank before they devaluated any further and change them into dollars. This was money from a Ukrainian sponsor for the *Messiah* concert. Roger knew that the bank had already taken 14 percent out as a service charge.

When Roger arrived at the bank to get the money, the lady said, "You have no money in that account."

"Yes, I do," said Roger, "just look at your computer screen." The lady coolly turned the screen toward him and, sure enough, it registered less than two dollars' worth of coupons, his initial deposit.

After much confusion and persistence, it was discovered that the two million coupons had been deposited in another person's account. To correct the mistake, the owner of the other account had to be contacted. It took some time, but finally Roger walked out of the bank with his 1,720,000 coupons, having paid an equivalent $23 service charge on $166.

The coupon had deflated from 8,500 to 12,000 (to the dollar) in the past three days. We had to spend these coupons fast before they disappeared. Changing them into dollars at the bank was unwise because of the terrible exchange rate there. The quickest way to save their value was to buy the furniture we needed. So we started visiting furniture stores. As I entered each store, I prayed,

"Please, Lord, let there be something here we can buy." But there was nothing! At least not the bedroom cupboards or hall cupboard that we needed to organize our belongings.

At 6:00 P.M. when the last store closed, we still had not spent the money. That night George McCammon saved us by purchasing the coupons for his Ukrainian payroll and giving us dollars instead. The next day the dollar was worth 13,000 coupons.

Dealing with the economic problems in Ukraine was a major frustration. Every transaction was in cash. There was no such thing as "writing a check" or getting receipts for a purchase. Inflation kept us guessing as to how much something might cost and what the figure might mean in terms of real money.

In these days, we rarely spent more than three dollars a week for groceries. Bread was two cents a loaf, but as inflation grew, it became ten cents a loaf. That frightened Ukrainian families. At the end of every month, it was almost impossible to find coupons for sale. Everyone was spending everything they had, anticipating that prices would rise again on the first of the month.

Having money was no guarantee that you could buy the food you wanted. As the warm temperatures disappeared, so did the availability of produce. Soon all we saw were potatoes, onions, cabbage, carrots, and beets, which are the ingredients for borscht. Apples were the only available fruit, left over from summer and stored underground.

The rest of our diet was a game of Russian roulette. It is true that meat was always available. We ate pork or beef. (The chickens were too tough to chew.) Sometimes we could find rice, but it would have to be cleaned and little rocks removed. Sugar and butter, necessary staples, would often disappear for days, or there would be a limit on how much you were allowed to buy. For a week we could find no eggs. Then there would be eggs, but no butter. Sugar was sometimes only available if you showed a document that said you lived in the region. It was like the Great Depression of the 1930s.

Other items such as lightbulbs and toilet paper were difficult to find, so I tried to buy them whenever I saw them.

Roger had recruited three Ukrainians to help him manage the business of our concerts. Even though the lacquering of floors kept us from living in our apartment, the daily work on our choir projects continued. Albert, a black man from Liberia whom the Communists had brought to Ukraine for indoctrination in Marxism four years ago, was really a Christian, spoke English, and had worked in George's office for a year. He was kindhearted, honest, and loyal to our work. He became our administrator and translated for us in business meetings.

Lydia Bychkova, a soprano soloist at the opera, had become our friend and offered to help Roger with musical connections and publicity. She spoke just a little English. She even sang in our choir until the Opera House rehearsals began and she became too busy. Our concerts were often planned around her solo talent: Brahms *Requiem*, Poulenc *Gloria*, and the opera *Amahl and the Night Visitors*.

Oksana Adamdenko, who also worked for George, typed our concert programs and translated letters. She had a difficult time accepting Roger's new capitalistic ideas.

One day Roger was talking about the difference in prices between America and Ukraine. The Opera House had rented gowns and tuxes to our choir for their *Messiah* performance for four hundred coupons a person (four cents, each), including cleaning and delivery. "Such a service in the United States would cost six dollars apiece just for the dry cleaning alone," Roger said. "But you must realize that in America it takes about $5,000 a month just to take care of the needs of a family. Many American families have two cars and sometimes three."

Oksana, her face red as a beet, blurted out, "That's why Ukraine is so poor! Americans have all the riches."

Roger, wanting to set her straight on her economics, said firmly, "No, Oksana, that is a lie you have been taught. There is not just one pie, and if I have a large slice, you have a small one. The pie grows. If I become rich, you can become richer because I can invest in things that will benefit you over a period of time."

It was hard to convince Oksana. She believed the reason banks existed was "to take your money."

We did not want to offend her, however. Not only was Oksana a talented translator with computer skills, but our apartment was also registered in her name. This meant that, according to the government, *she* was renting the flat, not foreigners, and *she* was the only one who could take the passbook and bring us sugar. Yes, sugar was rationed, even though Ukraine is the largest producer of sugar beets in the world.

We continued to look for the furniture we needed. Albert called to say that for $110 he had found a veneered cupboard set in a light blond color. We were excited.

On the way to see the furniture, we stopped in a clothing store. "I need a tie to go with my gray checked coat," Roger said. This was a government-owned clothing store. Most of the items were behind counters, and you had to ask to examine them. Roger saw a tie that looked just perfect. It was a solid gray color, and the width was just right. He asked to see it.

There were a bunch of numbers on the tag. He wasn't sure how to read the price. Roger gave the lady a 10,000 coupon bill (about eighty cents). She looked at him and gave the money back. Maybe she wanted more. He gave her a 20,000 coupon bill. Again she gave it back. She pointed to the 363 on the tag. The price must be 36,300 coupons ($3.05).

Roger was searching his billfold for more money when another shopkeeper came over to help. She started to put her fingers in his wallet. "No," said Roger as he pulled away. "I want to do this myself."

Finally, he found the 36,300 coupons and gave them to her. Then he noticed the antique cash register drawer contained only three, ten, and twenty-five coupon bills. The lady had been trying unsuccessfully to find change. Now he knew! The tie was only 363 coupons. He was willing to pay over $3, but it was only three cents! He took back his money, gave her the one thousand coupon bill, and told her to keep the change, which was seven cents.

We met Albert at the furniture store and approved the furniture, paying for it and arranging delivery on Friday. What a successful day it had been! Furniture and a three-cent tie!

Chapter 15
Odds and Ends

Friday was an exciting day. The apartment floors were finally dry from the last coat of lacquer. We said goodbye to the Hjelmfelds and reclaimed our apartment. Our friends helped us put the furniture back in place, and the new furniture arrived on schedule. We hadn't realized that we would have to put it together like a kit. But even so, it was good to be home.

For the next week, life was so easy. I made scheduled trips to the laundry in the school van and found a place for everything in the new shelves and drawers. I caught up with the many faxes to answer. I bought enough food to stock the cupboards and have a reasonable insurance against starvation. The new floors were just beautiful, the prettiest part of the whole apartment. I loved their slippery surface and shine.

We kept working on the apartment little by little. We hired two painters to sand and repaint the door frames that were caked with layers of paint sloppily applied. We bought the brushes and the paint. Unfortunately, the brushes were shaped like round powder puffs and the paint was watery. Sandpaper was nonexistent, let alone a power sanding tool. I found some sandpaper in our storage closet, and the painters did their best, which resulted in paint dripping on the newly polished floors. Finally, we paid them to leave.

We hired another man and his wife to wallpaper the kitchen. It took them five weeks to do a seven-foot square room, and that was only the top half above the tile. I paid them the $1-per-square-meter charge and breathed a sigh of relief when they left. I think it was their first attempt. They must have used scissors to trim the wallpaper next to the tile, because the edges were so ragged. I liked the pattern, however, which Stanislav and Albert had helped me to find. That search had taken three weeks.

We needed a private phone line. We shared our line with a family that had two teenage daughters. They were constantly on the phone outside of school hours. We could not hear their conversations. Instead, the phone would be dead until they hung up. Without a telephone line, we could not make business calls or even call for help in case of an emergency. A new line in our building would cost $200, and we finally decided it was necessary. We made the appointment and were prepared to pay the money. Albert waited at our apartment one night for three hours, but the workman never showed up. No matter how many times we tried to get our phone line, we were never successful.

Then we had some new problems. The telephone rates skyrocketed. When we first came to Kiev, the long distance rates to America were seven cents a minute. Now they had jumped to $2.50 a minute. Almost all of our communications were sent by fax. The phone lines were so terrible that at least one line per page was smeared. And sometimes the faxes would not transmit at all. Still, the government phone company charged plenty for use of the line. My transmission record said that of the fifty fax attempts in August, only twenty-three were successfully completed. Instead of an expected ten-dollar-a-month charge, we received a phone-line bill for 2,785,000 coupons (about $240).

With the devaluation of the coupon, however, the longer we waited to pay the bill, the lower the real price became. We had to guess how long we could wait without getting our phone line cut off.

We were still paying our choir members one dollar per rehearsal, but their pay was actually increasing because the dollar gained value every week. Soon we were the highest paying choir organization in the city.

Roger was in a dilemma with the choir rehearsals. The rehearsal room at the Polytechnical Institute was not adequate. We still had no storage place, and our enrollment was up to 105 singers. Since the school year had begun, it was also more difficult for Music Helen to host a visiting choir in her classroom.

We found a hall to rent for five dollars a night. It had 120 chairs and was in a central location in the city. We arranged to move there by the end of October. The room was located in a cultural arts building that we called the Bieli Dome, which means "white house." It was a white building with colorful ceramic tiles on the front. The large rehearsal room on the fourth floor was the home of a famous folk choir that used it during the day. We could use it at night. It had excellent acoustics, and they even gave us a library closet. We were in heaven.

At the first rehearsal we noticed that the bathrooms were large but had no toilet paper or soap. The next week I brought two large fluffy rolls of American toilet paper and two big bars of soap for the men's toilet on the second floor and the women's toilet on the third floor. At the beginning of rehearsal I placed them in the restrooms. But before intermission they had been stolen. Who would stoop so low as to steal toilet paper?

Next we tried two plastic bags with toilet paper and soap inside, placed by the door to the rehearsal room. But no one used them. Were they too shy? Or did they just prefer to carry their own? I usually did that—carry my own toilet paper everywhere I went. Roger kept a good supply in his briefcase. It was a necessary precaution.

One night Roger passed out questionnaires to the choir concerning scheduling:

1. Which nights are possible for you to rehearse?
2. Which nights are impossible for you to rehearse?
3. Which nights would you prefer to rehearse?

First Roger tried to explain the paper and have a discussion. The room exploded into shouts and arguing. "Wait!" Roger yelled, and they grew silent. "A discussion is listening to each other and expressing your opinion one at a time." But it was impossible!

Their only way to arrive at a decision was that the loudest one would decide for the group. The forms were filled out, but the results were so confusing that we threw them all in the wastebasket and set our own schedule. So much for democratic procedure!

Then a dreadful thing happened. Trying to artificially regulate the currency, the government announced that the dollar would be equal to 14,000 coupons as a fixed rate, not the 25,500 it had been. That meant that a dollar lost over 40 percent of its value, and our phone bill skyrocketed again from $234 to $400 in one day. In another first-time announcement, the government promised to double the state salaries of Ukrainians. This they eventually did, but the cost of living went up 700 percent. Their solution for an economic crisis in Ukraine was printing endless money, which continued to lose value.

Meanwhile we were having rehearsals and paying salaries on time. Whenever we had a concert, it would take all the money we had. We were broke. But then, miraculously, we would receive enough one dollar bills in greeting cards from our friends. Checking the mailbox at the local post office every week kept us fed.

On the day of the Brahms *Requiem* concert, I had counted out $900 in small bills for the orchestra in individual envelopes on the king-sized bed. I scooped them into my backpack and added a cheese sandwich for Roger, two bottles of Fanta orange drink, my black heels for the concert, and an umbrella and headed for the tram. By the time I boarded the tram, it had started to rain. Two miles later, the tram came to a stop. For a long time nothing happened. Passengers began to leave. What should I do? I was still five miles from the concert hall with $900 cash in my backpack. Should I hitchhike? I got off the car only to see three trams in front of ours also stopped. Must be an electrical failure. I stood there holding my umbrella in the drizzling rain. I didn't know how to tell a taxi where I was going in Russian. We were not far from the metro station. I would just walk along the track until I reached it. I had taken only a few steps when the first tram began to move. I ran back to the second tram and jumped aboard, thankful to have a ride in the rain to my next connection.

When I finally arrived at the theater, I took Roger his cheese sandwich and soda. He was less than pleased with my menu. It was better than his lunch that day, however. The director of the theater had taken him to his private dining room where he was forced to eat "sallow" (raw pig fat) on a slice of bread with a pickle. This is a Ukrainian delicacy but revolting to an American.

Leaving Roger's dressing room, I went into the hall to see many people arriving for the concert. As usual there were pending problems. The ushers were demanding double pay because it was a holiday. This meant an extra $24, which I fortunately had kept in my billfold. Bogdana and Oksana came in with some friends, and I immediately put them to work passing out the programs. The ushers were invisible. Not one was passing out programs or showing people to their seats. I wanted to complain, but there was no one to report to, and I could not speak the language. I had just paid double salary and no one was working! I was steaming as I stomped toward the lobby. There I saw Humanitarian Helen, standing at the main door passing out programs. Good!

Soon the hall was filled with Ukrainians as well as foreigners: the Norwegian ambassador, the ambassador of Argentina, members of the English embassy, and a committee from the United Nations. George McCammon offered an opening prayer and the concert began.

The audience sat spellbound at the beauty of Brahms. Lydia Bychkova and Stanislav Pavlenko were marvelous in their solos. This was the first Brahms *Requiem* presented in Ukraine—the entire text is scripture about the reality of death and the hope of the resurrection in Jesus Christ. Sung in German, the text was printed in Ukrainian and English in the program for the audience—words that shall endure forever.

After the performance, we packed a suitcase full of ten coats and trousers that we had brought for the men of the chorus who had no performance clothes. Then, with the orchestra music and one hundred extra programs for the office file, we walked down the hill in the icy, cold air and hailed a taxi. "How much money do you have left?" asked Roger after we paid the driver.

"Four dollars," I said.

"Well, that's enough for tomorrow," he said. He was right. We were living on "manna."

Chapter 16
A Star Named Lydia

Lydia Bychkova was doing a wonderful job connecting us to the cultural leaders in Ukraine. Not only had we had a successful performance of the Brahms *Requiem* at the Franko Theater, but we also had scheduled the Durufle *Requiem* at the Dome Organi Musiki and the Spirituals Concert at the Tchaikovsky Conservatory Hall—all in the month of November.

Lydia invited us to her apartment for dinner one night. She had been given this apartment by President Krafchuk when he heard her performance in *Prince Igor,* an opera by Borodin. Her home was located in a modern highrise building surrounded by other new buildings where many of the government leaders resided. I was impressed by the clean glass doors at the entrance and the new elevators. *This must be a great apartment for Ukraine,* I thought.

Sergei Basarab had come with us even though he had had an exhausting day of work at the Norwegian embassy. Though Lydia spoke some English, there were times when we could not communicate without help.

Lydia opened the door and warmly greeted us. "You are the first guests I have had since I moved to this apartment," she said.

What we saw inside was not what we had expected. There was practically no furniture in the apartment. She had a twin bed in the one room and a table and one stool in the kitchen. The apartment was basically unfinished: no door knobs on the doors, no cupboards in the kitchen, and the drain to the bathroom sink did not attach to the floor. The small refrigerator did not work, and she was using the windowsill to keep her food cool. The apartment had no telephone, and it would cost $500 to have a line installed.

The main room had no light due to faulty wiring. Lydia had a lightbulb screwed into a long cord that plugged into the outlet in the hall. She pulled the cord into the dark room so we could see where she lived. Everything Lydia owned was in heaps upon the floor, including her most precious possession: a collection of LP albums of music. Her record player had been broken for some time.

We were so saddened by her condition. This wonderful lady, who is such a great opera singer, was living in poverty. With a monthly salary of seven dollars, she could afford no furniture.

Yet Lydia was so happy to have her friends visit. She was busily preparing dinner for us in the kitchen. She moved the table to the center of the room and cleared it. Since there were no cupboards, it also functioned as her work space and storage space for her limited dinnerware and kitchen utensils. She gave me her stool to sit on, and she and Roger sat on boxes. The plastic stool that supported her useless refrigerator was removed to provide Sergei a seat.

As we began to enjoy her delicious food, Sergei's stool collapsed and, with a look of utter horror, he floated to the floor. We couldn't help laughing. Sergei, who had appeared so tired from his long day of work, was now wide awake. Lydia apologized profusely. I tried not to laugh, for her sake, but I could not hold back my laughter.

After dinner Lydia would not let me help with the dishes. She wanted to give Roger recordings. She wanted to knit me a hat. Her entire focus was on giving to us. We were her friends, and she could not do enough.

Most of all, she wanted to return to America and earn some money with her singing so that she could better her situation in Ukraine. She had been there in March, at our invitation, to sing Verdi's *Requiem* at our church in Orlando. She had stayed at our home in Winter Park.

Standing there in her apartment, now I understood her amazement at the little things in American life. When we had driven into our driveway, Roger pushed the garage door opener and the door lifted for our car to enter. "Impossible!" she had said, shaking her head. After settling into our guest room, she went outside into the backyard filled with flowers. "Is this all for *you?*" she had asked innocently.

Following her performance at our church, she went to New York City where she auditioned at the Metropolitan Opera, interviewed with Columbia Artists, and later stood in the wings at Carnegie Hall as an understudy for a performer who was barely able to complete her performance. Lydia's visit was cut short by the necessity to return to Ukraine where her elderly mother who was in poor health lived in a small village.

Now back in Ukraine she was again working at the Opera House, frustrated and unappreciated. She said that she was not given many leading roles because she was Russian. Others would say that she was impossible to work with, given her explosive artistic temperament. All I knew was that she had the most beautiful soprano voice that I had ever heard.

We were her fans when we attended the Opera. After the performance we always went backstage to her dressing room. There she would be in all her glory in a gorgeous gown, sometimes wearing a crown and fancy jewelry. Then, behind the screen, the costume ladies would remove her wig, jewelry, gown, and tiara—and she would don her sweatshirt and slacks, becoming "Eliza Doolittle" again. There was no one to say, "Great job! Beautiful performance!" She brought her own cake and tea and served us refreshments in an after-show celebration. Then she packed everything, including the spoons, into her knapsack and headed for the public transportation, returning to her one-room apartment, alone and unnoticed.

Ever since I had visited Lydia's apartment, I wanted to get her some furniture. I had no money, but I wrote some friends in America and they raised $110 for a cupboard set. It was still not enough to buy a whole set of shelves, cupboards, and drawers. I knew that Lydia adored our new blond veneer cupboards, so I determined to give it to her and buy us another set. Prices were going up, however. Another set would cost us more than the first one, but I could afford to pay more than Lydia. How long would it take her to save the difference in price at seven dollars a month in wages?

Lydia was delighted to hear news about the donors in America and receive our furniture for it. She insisted on helping us buy another one for ourselves by accompanying us to the House of Furniture, the largest furniture store in town. This store was a huge pavilion with a roofline that resembled a flying bat. There were two floors of furniture displays. The lower floor had expensive imported furniture, and the upper floor had Ukrainian furniture. We found a veneer cabinet set upstairs that would blend with the pecan headboard of our bed. It was not as pretty as the first set, but it would be functional. The most important fact was that it was available that day to buy.

With Lydia we went through all the red tape of buying it, a process that took three hours. By the time we were finished, having signed the last paper and paid the last coupon, I had nicknamed the store the "House of Nightmares." Roger had also bought Lydia a new table for helping us at the furniture store. It was only eleven dollars. During the next few years, we returned to the House of Nightmares. Even though I hated the process, it gave us the best products for our money.

Lydia loved to visit our apartment. She called it a palace, which I took as a joke the first time she said it. But compared to her living situation, it was. She taught me how to make borscht and often brought me cakes. I, in turn, brought her my sweaters or dresses that were too big for me, as my frame was shrinking from so much exercise. She was so happy to receive these American clothes that she grabbed me and lifted me up off the ground, saying, "Thank you! Thank you!"

When Lydia helped us arrange concerts, they were concerts that usually featured herself as the soprano soloist. She had a persuasive manner and worked hard to make these concerts happen. We scheduled Menotti's one-act opera *Amahl and the Night Visitors* that season at the Conservatory. She played the role of the poor mother who envied the gold of the Three Wise Men and tried to steal some for her crippled son. The desperation of the character of the mother was mirrored in Lydia herself. She was a desperately deprived person—deprived of love, money, and recognition for her talent. Though many people complained about Lydia's aggressiveness and irritability, I felt a special compassion for her. She was a star whose brightness was all but extinguished by a cold and cruel system. Lydia would have been recognized as a world-class soprano soloist, but she had been born behind the Iron Curtain. And for Lydia, at forty-eight years of age, the dawn of freedom came almost too late.

Chapter 17

An Open Door

One of the principal objectives of our work in Ukraine was to become involved with the Ukrainian people. It is easy to isolate oneself in a circle of American friends. From the very beginning, however, our home was open to the Ukrainians we met.

Every Tuesday night we scheduled a Bible class that Roger taught. At first we met at George's school. Albert came, also Oksana, and two men and three ladies from the church. One woman named Luda had been a KGB spy, but now she professed to be a Christian. We formed the class to teach others how to share their faith. But mostly we were explaining about faith itself.

After a few weeks, the class moved to our living room. Some choir members began to attend. Sasha Sikorsky (Preacher Sasha) became our regular translator. In the next few months many people visited. Some brought their friends or relatives to hear teachings about the Scriptures, some became Bible scholars, and some came to faith in Christ.

Albert, our Liberian administrator, was a regular at the Bible study. One night he shared his testimony. As a teenager in Liberia, Albert was a rebel. Every time he walked past the church, he felt a deep guilt about his life. Soon he even avoided coming near the church. One day he and his best friend were discussing the emptiness they felt in their lives. They decided to go into the church and try to find God and His forgiveness for their rebellious behavior. Albert became acquainted with some Christian musicians, and God used them to bring Albert to Himself. From that time on, he knew that Jesus is with him.

Albert has suffered much. His daughter died of starvation in Liberia, and his wife was put in a concentration camp. His wife finally was released and is living in England, but she has informed him that she wants a divorce. He was brought to Ukraine by the Communists who wanted to train intelligent young black men in Marxism. Now he was free to return to his country, but because of the war there, his life would be in danger. Still he wanted to return to his homeland. The money he earned from us would help to get him home.

Diana Milevska, a blonde soprano in our choir, volunteered to share her story. Diana was faithful in a Communist youth organization. She had always loved music and was attracted by the music she heard coming from her village church. One Sunday morning she decided to visit the church. She even dared to come the next week. This time, however, a Communist group came into the church and dragged her out. She was disciplined and told never to go into that church again. Then, years later, she saw an advertisement in the Kiev paper for singers to join American conductor Roger McMurrin in learning Western classical church music. She auditioned and sang Handel's *Messiah* with us in 1992. Through the experience of the music and the prayers and teaching of this American conductor, she came to Christ and her life was changed.

The Bible class lasted an hour and a half, beginning with hymn singing and closing with prayer followed by refreshments. Often, just as we were closing, the visitors began asking questions that had been on their hearts all evening. "How do you prepare yourself to be saved?" "Why should we pray when God already knows what we want?" "Why was blood necessary in Old Testament sacrifices?"

We patiently tried to explain what the Bible said about these questions. These were not questions of cynicism. They were questions of searching. Sasha Donskoy sat in our class for almost a year. Sasha was not a believer, but he kept coming, kept listening. His only response was, "We were not taught these things under

Communism." With his dark hair, brown eyes, and black moustache, Sasha sat there stroking his chin, thinking. Even with his stiff resistance to the Gospel, God was preparing him for a great change in his life.

Valentina Yenichek, another new choir member, started coming weekly to Bible study. She was a short little blonde who had grown up in an orphanage. As an orphan, she was not allowed to go to church. When we met her, she was forty years old and in her second marriage. She came to the Bible study because her heart was burdened for her daughter who had become part of a local religious group that was teaching "beating with a heavy belt" was an acceptable discipline for children. Valentina wanted to know more about the Bible in order to counsel her daughter and dissuade her from the church's teachings. Valentina had never felt comfortable in any church, but within the Bible study group she learned who God was, that He loved her, and that it was by His grace that He offers salvation. For a year and a half, she sat in the class, learning, praying, and feeling His light in her soul.

Larisa the Blonde came regularly too. She loved studying the Bible and grew in her understanding of God's Word. Her pathway of faith took her back to the Orthodox Church where she preferred to worship. God brought peace to her heart there, she said, and she attended regularly.

Irina Loktionova, who had been in our 1992 choir, was faithful at our Bible classes. She was incredibly honest concerning her spiritual condition. In her first visit, she responded to the question "Do you know for sure that you are going to heaven?" by saying, "No, I'm going to hell." There was a sadness about Irina. She was separated from her husband, who was studying at the University in Moscow. When the Soviet Union dissolved, he was trapped there, and Irina was in Kiev. They had a young son, and Irina's husband found it difficult to visit them often. He chose to finish his education instead of caring for his family. The situation eventually ended in a divorce, with Irina supporting their child on her meager salary from a state choir plus what she earned singing with us. After attending our Bible study for a year, Irina wrote the following note to us:

I am so grateful to you, Diana and Roger, that your Bible classes bring so much to our souls, which want to find the truth but cannot find it anywhere except in the Word of God. I know now that the Bible can answer any of my questions and helps me in everyday life. It gives me peace and comfort, but sometimes I am so sad that, seeing the pattern I should be, I do not very often respond to it. And you know the struggle in my heart. Your lesson helps me to do small steps in the right way. When I suffer, I remember that no one's pain was greater than Christ's. When I have joy, I am sure that God shares with me His joy.

It's our greatest sin when we rebel against God because of our pride, when we are not meek and poor in spirit. Sometimes we are sure that we deserve a better life, and we think that God was unjust to us. In this way we rebel against God, and the same moment the devil comes to us and crucifies our souls with his assistants—jealously, anger, hatred, etc. He forms a small "hell" inside us and destroys our soul. The only way to struggle against it is shown in Scriptures.

I am sure that your help in our study of the Bible, your prayers for us, and the Holy Spirit who is present at your classes support us and make us better. Your lessons made me realize that I should not only be "salt" because I argue with other people about the faith, but I must have more patience. Very often I cannot bring the "light" because I don't know the Bible well, and it is impossible for me to explain to them the truth it brings. What a pity that many people are not seeking God! They avoid this greatest light, which will show how sinful they are, and they don't believe that the gospel brings the great joy of God's salvation.

Your classes always give peace to my heart because you keep saying: "Jesus loves you. Don't give up. Trust in God. Love Him, and it will change your life."

Our living room seated fourteen people in a tight squeeze. Every week the room was full but not necessarily with the same people. We knew that God was using that gathering to accomplish His purposes. We were loving and available to our people, teaching them what we knew of the Lord's way and sharing our experiences of faith with them. The Gospel was always present in our teachings.

God's promise is: "You have been faithful with a few things; I will put you in charge of many things" (Matt. 25:21). Little did we know how many things the Lord would give us in the years to follow. At that time we offered ourselves daily to His work, whatever it would be, and trusted Him for the results. In less than three months, that little Bible study would begin to affect hundreds of lives in a direction we never dreamed to be possible.

Chapter 18
A Little Child Shall Lead Them

Sasha was a Jew who had married a Russian girl. Neither family was religious. The marriage was arranged by the parents, and the bride and groom met for the first time one week before the wedding. "This girl is smart," Sasha's parents told him. "She is wholesome. She will make a good wife for you."

To escape persecution as a Jew, Sasha assumed the surname of his wife, Lena Donskaya. He became Sasha Donskoy. All Russian names for women end in the vowel *a*, a variant of the husband's or father's name. From their wedding pictures, they were a strikingly attractive couple.

Sasha and Lena had two children; first, Andre, a son, and then Dasha, a daughter. At the dawn of Ukrainian independence in 1991, Dasha was six years old and ready to begin elementary school. A new curriculum was offered called ACE (Accelerated Christian Education). Lena, who was an elementary school vice-principal, examined the curriculum and saw that it was an excellent educational tool, not only teaching the traditional academic subjects in an interesting way but also introducing English as a spoken and written language for children. The classes would be taught in English, an excellent opportunity for their daughter. She filled out the application, and Dasha was accepted into the program.

When Dasha brought her first books home, she was not only reading English but also Bible verses concerning moral ethics and Jesus' teachings. Day after day she read the verses and asked questions. As parents, Sasha and Lena felt unequipped to answer her questions. They had both been brought up as atheists, and they had never read the Bible. They began reading the Scripture in Russian to help their daughter. Sasha thought it taught good principles for his daughter to learn. Lena began to study English too, thinking it would be helpful not only for her daughter's education but also for her own.

One day, instead of a teachers' meeting, a team of missionaries from a group called Co-Mission came to speak. They introduced material called "Curriculums about Christian Morals and Ethics."

This book helped Lena answer so many questions of the teenagers in her school. Missionaries came to the school to volunteer as teachers for the program. In the early 1990s this was permissible, but later American missionaries were no longer allowed by law to teach the Bible in the classroom. Co-Mission began to train Ukrainian teachers, so that they could continue to teach this curriculum. Lena attended the conference, and through the nine days of intensive training she became a Christian, asking Christ into her heart.

Sasha continued to study the Bible because he wanted to learn more about the greatest literature piece of all time, to read the history of the Jewish people, and to guide his daughter in her studies. Before the breakup of the Soviet Union, Sasha had been a sergeant in the Soviet Army, working with strategic missiles. Later he was an engineer at a military radio plant that produced electronic systems for nuclear weapons that were pointed at the United States. When Ukraine became an independent state, Sasha left the plant and began working in the State Property Foundation (the Ministry of Privatization).

It was at this time that we met Sasha Donskoy. Dasha was in her third year with the ACE program, but now the parents had to pay tuition. Sasha and Lena enjoyed going to dancing class together several nights a week. It was their special time with each other. In order to pay Dasha's tuition, Sasha would have to give up the dancing classes and find a second job.

Sasha had heard that there was an American conductor in town who was looking for singers. He paid one dollar per rehearsal. If Sasha could join the choir, he could afford to keep Dasha in the special program. In September 1993, he came to Roger McMurrin to audition.

Sasha had no professional training like the other candidates, but he was very smart and he could sight-read anything. Roger also liked his personality: confident, direct, and friendly. He accepted Sasha into the choir, and the rehearsals, four nights a week, had a great impact upon Sasha's life.

He sang music that was written to the glory of God. It amazed him. Roger talked openly about God and the Scripture. This "spiritual music" touched him deeply, and he became more drawn to learn about God. Sasha started coming to our Bible study, first alone. Then he brought his wife. Lena was all smiles when she sat with him on Tuesday nights. I knew that she must be a Christian by her comments and her countenance.

When the Church of the Holy Trinity began in 1994, Lena was one of the first people to request baptism. Sasha was glad for her and attended her baptism, but he still held back. He did request that his children be baptized, however. He started bringing Andre and Dasha to our Bible study.

Andre at this time became a Christian, largely because of Dasha's witness to him. "It happened so very smoothly that we did not even notice it," said Sasha. But now both children were responding to the Bible lessons and contributing with the others, their beautiful faces shining and alive.

Later that summer Dasha and Andre were baptized. Sasha watched. After that day, Andre wanted to be called Andrew. And to us, that was his name.

In the fall we decided to register our little church that had been meeting for almost eight months. By government law, we needed to elect a president and a treasurer. We selected Edward Senko, our orchestra manager, to become the president. He was willing to take the responsibility of signing legal papers and taking care of documents. We did not know whom we could ask to be treasurer.

We gathered a group of five women and five men to officially start the church. We asked Sasha Donskoy to attend the meeting. Although we knew he was not yet a believer, he had been so faithful at the Bible studies and had been faithfully attending the worship services. Sasha had helped with ticket sales for the concerts and kept very accurate records. Every jot and tittle was correct. We asked him to be the church treasurer, and he accepted. Yes, at the time he was a declared atheist, but he was honest and a good bookkeeper. He knew atheism was not the answer. He just hadn't become a Christian yet.

It was almost Christmas 1995. We were getting ready to go back to America for a Christmas break. The last of our little Tuesday night Bible studies was being held in the Bereznikee apartment. When we returned we would be moving into a new apartment in the center of the city. How nice it would be to have larger quarters. It would be a new era. The night before we left for the United States, Sasha gave Roger a sealed envelope which Roger put in his briefcase. On the airplane Roger opened the letter and read, "I know you will find this hard to believe, but I have become a Christian. I thank you for leading the way for me. I believe in Jesus Christ, and I want to serve Him."

The following May, Sasha received his baptism in the Dnieper River as a new believer. He was wearing a white shirt with the name of Jesus printed many times in every color of the rainbow. The family was complete in Christ. And it all started with a little six-year-old girl as she began to read the Bible.

The next year Sasha Donskoy was not only our church treasurer but our administrator as well. He left his privatization job to work full time for Roger and Music Mission Kiev. In the spring he took Roger and me on a picnic with his whole family, including his mother, father, brother, and his family. It was his father's seventieth birthday.

Sasha and Lena picked us up in his 1964 Moskvich antique car and drove to a forest outside of Kiev. There we made *shish kebabs* and enjoyed many homemade salads as we sat on blankets outstretched on the forest floor. It was a very hot day, and we drank water flavored with rose petals. Sasha took out his accordion (*bayon*) and played Ukrainian music while the family brought their 1887 *samovar*, a silver pot that heats water for tea. The children gathered pine cones, which were placed in the center metal tube of the *samovar*. Then a match lit the cones, which created great heat. The smoke came rolling out the portable chimney. The fire heated the water to a boil, and the smoke kept away the mosquitoes. Then the chimney was removed and a small teapot was placed on the top. From this was served very strong tea to be diluted by the hot water in the body of the *samovar*.

It was a relaxing afternoon . . . listening to music, playing badminton, walking in the woods, taking a nap under a birch tree. "Sasha and I knew nothing about the Bible before you and Roger came," said Lena to me as we sat together watching the children play. "Our lives are different now."

It was a day when we became friends with the entire family and felt accepted by them.

Sasha and Lena went on our tour to America in 1996. Sasha sang, and Lena served as translator and sold programs at the concerts, wearing a Ukrainian costume. Staying in twenty different American homes taught them a lot—about America and about the Christian life. They made many friends and looked forward to building a church like they saw in America.

When they returned to Kiev, Lena went back to her job as vice-principal at School #182. She administrated and sometimes taught in the ACE program that was still functioning in her school. There were two classes now, and she hoped to expand that into more, perhaps a whole elementary program that taught only Accelerated Christian Education.

We were concerned that not many children were attending our church, which met on Sunday afternoons. Helen suggested that we have a children's Sunday school on Saturday at her school, where many children live close by in the neighborhood. "I know many children. I could invite them to come on Saturdays as an extra activity and learn about the Bible," she said. We called this our underground Saturday Bible school. Because we were using a public school to meet, we had to give it other names every six weeks. Lena knew Christian teachers who wanted to help. The children came and the classes grew. Raisa, an extraordinary teacher, had fifty students in her class of first through fourth graders. She entertained them with Bible stories, sometimes illustrated with a flannel board. The children enjoyed games about the Bible—with prizes for the winners— crafts, memory exercises, and lots of love.

Andrew (formerly Andre) learned English so well that he began translating the Tuesday afternoon Bible study at our home. Roger began teaching a class on Saturday mornings with Andrew's classmates at School #182 called "The Influence of Christ on Western Culture," which was part of the regular school curriculum. Andrew was his translator and assistant.

Dasha grew older and continued her studies in the ACE program. As she became a teenager, she influenced many children at her school who considered her to be a leader. I still have the letter she wrote in English at the age of eight, before her father became a Christian. It reads:

Dear friends,

My name is Dasha Donskaya. I am 8.5 years old. I live in Kiev with my mother, father, grandmother, grandfather, and brother. My father sings at the choir of Roger. We are going on his concerts with whole family. I like this music very much.

I am studying in Christian private class by American program called "Accelerated Christian Education." All people of Kiev are interested in music of Roger's concerts. I know it because all the tickets are sold all the time. I know that Roger's friends from USA send him money. Roger gives salary to singers and musicians. My father receives some pay too. Therefore I can study at my school and pay for it. I am very thankful to you, and I want to say that friends of Roger are my friends too.

Dasha

Sasha continued to come to work weekdays at our apartment, handling the business of the concerts. He worked until 6:00 P.M. every night. Then three nights a week he would go immediately to choir practice. Perhaps no other person was so immersed in the mission work of the McMurrins as Sasha Donskoy. He was far from his former job of creating electronic systems for nuclear missiles aimed at the United States. Says Sasha of that experience, "Thank God, after Ukraine became an independent state, this nightmare was stopped forever. My evolution from an atheist and a soldier-enemy of the USA to the friend of America and one of the active members of the Church of the Holy Trinity is the best evidence of the Lord's power and glory!"

Chapter 19

The Miracle of
the First Christmas

It was November 1993. We had been living in Kiev for only four months, but we had already presented five concerts. Though we never knew how much money we had received until the thirtieth of every month, we held rehearsals and planned concerts in faith that the money would be there when the bills had to be paid. By the twenty-fifth, I was having anxiety attacks wondering if, indeed, the money would come. Finally, when we would get the list of contributors, there would be just enough money to cover our commitments. Because we had no savings to fall back on, we were completely dependent on the Lord's provision.

We knew that my mother would be giving fifty dollars from her social security. Roger's mother would provide one hundred dollars, and Roger's cousin Evelyn would keep sending fifty dollars a month. There were eight other friends who contributed equal or lesser amounts. Our monthly payroll for the choir was over $1600 a month, however. (One dollar per rehearsal for each singer and four rehearsals a week.) Amazingly every month we received gifts from unexpected sources to cover the costs.

In a monthly, twenty-page publication called *Chronicles of Kiev*, I was sending my journal writings to all who gave an average of twenty-five dollars a month. These pages were sent by fax to Nancy, our volunteer in Orlando, Florida, who retyped and printed them into a booklet. The mailing list was periodically revised, reaching seventy-five to a hundred people.

In mid-November Roger came home and told me he had made a decision about Christmas. We were going to present our Christmas concert three times. I was shocked and angry. "We don't have enough money for three concerts. We're already doing Poulenc's Gloria and the Spirituals Concert this month. Even if our friends are generous, there is *no way* to give more than one concert in the first two weeks of December." (We were going to America for a break on December 10.)

"It's our first Christmas. The hall seats only 700 people. We *have* to give this concert three times. It is a waste to present all this lovely Christmas music just once," Roger said.

I went to the rehearsal that night, taking attendance as usual. At the end of the rehearsal Roger told the choir, "My wife is upset with me. I have committed to presenting this Christmas concert three times. We have money for only one concert. But I believe this is what God wants. We are going to form a circle and pray for God's help. Even if you are not a believer, I ask that you join the circle while I pray."

The choir members obediently came to the center of the room and made a large circle. Holding hands, the circle was unbroken as Roger prayed, "Lord, we ask that You would provide for these concerts so that Your name may be glorified through this beautiful music that tells of Your coming into the world. May all Ukraine know of Your love and grace."

That night around 2:00 A.M., the phone rang. It was a fax. Nancy in Orlando sent us a letter from a new donor who had enclosed a check for $5,000. It was the largest donation we had ever received, and it was just enough for the remaining two Christmas concerts. We were ecstatic. It was hard to sleep that night. Truly this was an answer to prayer.

Two days later at the next rehearsal Roger announced to the choir how their prayer had been answered. From that time on, there was a new interest in this God whom Roger spoke of so frequently. We scheduled the concerts at the Dome Organi Musiki for December 2, 6, and 9.

After the first concert, the front page headline in a popular former-Communist newspaper was "Jesus Christ Is Born Forever" with a picture of Roger conducting, arms outspread and mouth open as if he himself were speaking the words. The reporter had done an extended piece on the concert, quoting the lyrics of the carols, which had been printed in the Ukrainian-English program. The title of the article seemed to be a combination of the carols and the "Hallelujah Chorus" that ended the concert. Though the first concert had been sold out, the next two had "standing room only" crowds as well.

The concerts were not without struggles, however. Before the second concert, the electrician told us that if we did not pay him a bribe, he would turn out the lights at intermission and not allow the concert to continue. We knew that paying one bribe would lead to others, and soon we would be enslaved by whoever approached us. We did not pay. Instead we prayed, and the man did not turn out the lights.

Igor Kushikov, a baritone in the choir who spoke English, was deeply touched by the concert. At the end, he came to Roger with tears in his eyes, saying, "Now I know what Christmas is all about " By his own testimony, Christ came into his life that night. He was singing "O Little Town of Bethlehem," and the tears started to fall

How silently, how silently, the blessed gift is given,
So God imparts to human hearts the blessings of His heaven.
No ear may hear His coming, but in this world of sin,
Where meek souls will receive Him still
The dear Christ enters in.

After the third performance, we came back to the apartment and stayed up all night to pack. Tomorrow we would leave on the train for Budapest. We had thirty-two dollars left in our pocket after paying the Christmas concert expenses. With our credit cards and a few unused traveler's checks (useless in Ukraine), we could make it through Munich to catch our plane to America.

During the three weeks in America, we would need to raise the funds to return. But having seen what the Lord had done, it was easier to trust Him to continue the work. He had certainly revealed to us that He was in charge.

Early the next morning before dawn, we were ready to board the train when we saw a familiar face. It was Larisa the Blonde. She had come to wish us "safe voyage" and had brought some home-made jam—just what I needed for the bread that I was carrying for the train. We hugged and kissed and waved goodbye as the train pulled away from the station heading west.

Twenty-five hours later we were in Budapest. It felt familiar by now, the fourth time we had seen the station. We went to the little office that displayed the American Express sign and purchased the tickets for Munich. We cashed one of our traveler's checks and headed for McDonald's.

We were deliriously happy as we ordered our breakfast, like we had just come to visit old friends. Big Macs for breakfast tasted wonderful. In the windows of McDonald's and across the overhead menu were Christmas lights and tinsel.

Eleven hours later we arrived at the Munich train station. Walking through the bustling terminal, we exited to a street that was ablaze with Christmas lights. Across the boulevard, little white lights outlined every sparkling clean window, covering the whole building in orderly array. "It is so *beautiful*," I said, holding back the tears. We stood there hypnotized by the lights, gazing in awe, as others passed by without looking. It was a moment of pure joy, a rediscovery of a culture that radiated hope and beauty and dignity. We were in the West!

Chapter 20

A Church Is Born

When we returned in January, we received news that our request for 150 Bibles had been answered. On January 16, Roger passed out a Bible to every choir member at rehearsal. He was not prepared for the level of excitement they displayed. It was as if we had given them new cars. A Bible through the black market in Communist times had been worth three months' wages. Now it was a free gift. Roger spent an hour autographing the Bibles personally to each person who asked.

Knowing of their enthusiasm, Sergei Basarab asked Roger, "The people want to know when are we going to start classes so that we can understand this book." Though Sergei was an agnostic, he kept asking the question, as much for himself as for the others. Each rehearsal the question was repeated. Then the question became "When are we going to start this *church?*"

Roger kept saying, "I'm not ready yet." What he meant was that he felt he should find a Ukrainian pastor to lead them in their own language. He had Sasha Sikorsky (Preacher Sasha) in mind. Roger and I had attended the church he was pastoring and saw that Sasha had a gift for preaching and a great following there, especially among the children. Sasha, whose father had deserted the family when he was very young, considered Roger to be his father figure and even called him "Dad."

Roger told Sasha, "All I'm asking you to do is to preach in the afternoon the same message you gave in the morning. Come and teach them God's Word." But Sasha was hesitant. His church was mostly children, some women, and a few men. Roger was asking him to come to a group of very educated adults who might be skeptical atheists. He was reluctant, but finally he agreed to come.

On the last Saturday of January we held a party for the choir at the Bratislava Hotel: a full dinner and evening of shared entertainment for 240 people. The purpose of the party was to thank the choir for the wonderful work they had given since August and to announce the beginning of our church services the following week. Five days before the party, a Canadian businessman had visited our rehearsal. When he heard about the upcoming party, he asked Roger, "How much does something like that cost?" "Six hundred dollars," Roger replied, to which the man took out his wallet and handed Roger six crisp one hundred dollar bills.

The party was a huge success. Each choir member brought a spouse or special friend, and Roger and I greeted each family and had a photo taken together, which we later gave them as a souvenir. The choir members organized the entertainment program among themselves, and it was a great show. They departed that night full of gratitude for this special event. Most of the singers had never been to a restaurant. It was a landmark experience.

A week later the first worship service was held in our rehearsal room. About one hundred people from the banquet attended. We had a printed worship order and some photocopied hymns. Sasha preached on the Messiah, referring to many scriptures from the musical work they knew: who Jesus is, what He did on the cross, and finally is He *your* Messiah?

At the end of the sermon, Sasha bravely said, "If you want to receive Jesus Christ as your Savior this day, I want you to stand." Ninety people stood up and prayed to receive salvation. The next week fourteen more came forward to accept Christ. Our church was born.

Though many of the new believers had been baptized in the Orthodox Church as young children, several had never received the sacrament of baptism. They requested to be baptized. Sasha Sikorsky, like many Ukrainians, believed the only place to be baptized was in the Dnieper River. By June the water temperature was tolerable for our first baptism service.

On a Sunday afternoon about two o'clock, we gathered on an island in the middle of the Dnieper River by a grove of trees and held a worship service. It was a small group, about twenty. We sang hymns, prayed, and were instructed about baptism. Six people spoke their vows of belief in Christ and walked one by one into the river with Sasha to be baptized. Their faces were radiant as they came out of the water.

Lena Donskaya, Sasha Donskoy's wife, was baptized in that group. Valentina Yenichek, our little blonde ray of sunshine, also came out of the water aglow. Eugenia Maksimova, our business lady-choir singer, walked into the water, braided hairpiece and all, and was baptized. "Now I have a new life in Christ," she said, smiling.

Lydia Bychkova was present at the service but whispered to me, "Diane, I want to be baptized, but I just got out of the hospital with pneumonia. I want to wait until the water is warmer."

Then we went to the rehearsal hall where the congregation was gathering for worship. It would be our first communion. About eighty people were present. After a beautiful service, Sasha presented the sacrament to us. A violin played a Bach air. The people formed a long line to receive the elements, and Roger assisted Sasha by holding the chalice of wine in which the bread was dipped, and the people partook. As Roger saw each face come before him, he was overcome with emotion, realizing this was the first time for many to receive this sacrament—new creatures in Christ. Tears began to drip down his cheeks. He had difficulty wiping them away.

At the end of the communion, Roger whispered to Sasha, "Did Sergei Basarab take communion?" Sasha shook his head no. Roger then went forward to lead the closing hymn. During the singing, Sasha approached Sergei and said, "Did you want to take communion?"

"I have not been baptized," said Sergei.

"If you believe in Jesus Christ as Savior and Lord, it is permissible to participate in communion."

"I believe," said Sergei. And Sasha administered communion to him during the last verse of the hymn.

After the service Roger was surprised to hear that Sergei had received communion. We invited Sergei over for dinner the following Saturday, anxious to hear about what had happened in his life. After dinner, we asked him, "Sergei, what was it that led to your belief in Christ? Was it a particular scripture you read or heard? Was it the writings of C. S. Lewis that we gave you for Christmas?"

Sergei looked solemnly to Roger. "No, it was none of that." He paused and then quietly replied, "It was your tears."

The young intellectual had been touched not by words but by the Spirit. God had used Roger's tears at that communion service to touch Sergei's heart, and Jesus became real in his mind and soul.

Chapter 21
The Unexpected

One of the lessons of Ukraine is "Expect the unexpected." In January 1995 we received a box from America. Inside were homemade Christmas cookies and a note. The three of us immediately sampled the eight different kinds of cookies. Some tasted better than others. Upon reading the note, I came to the phrase, "It was nice to visit with your son Marc last week." I knew that Marc had not been in that home for over a year. It became clear that these cookies had been circulating in the Ukrainian postal system for not fourteen days but rather fourteen months. The cookies we had eaten were over a year old!

The Ukrainian postal system did bring rewards, however. Our friends used to send one dollar bills enclosed in greeting cards. Because the mailbox in our building was permanently broken, we collected our mail at the neighborhood post office. I carried my chunky little key, but Roger said anything would open our box: a tiny screwdriver or the edge of a knife. We were never robbed, to the best of our knowledge.

Our friends were careful to send *new* one dollar bills. If they were marked, torn, taped, or older than that 1988 issue, Ukraine considered them "worthless." We had a pile of "worthless" bills to take back to America twice a year. Whenever we returned to Kiev, we brought back between one thousand and two thousand one-dollar bills, since they were impossible to find in Ukraine. If we could not get new bills from American banks, we would have to inspect them all, usually rejecting 20 percent.

I visited the post office about three times a week. Usually I would read my letters while I walked, sometimes stumbling on the broken sidewalks as a result. If there was cash enclosed, I carefully folded the bills and slipped them into my coat pocket as secretly as any magician, for there were eyes everywhere. If someone suspected that money was arriving in our mailbox, that would be the end of it.

One day I was particularly weary and sad. In our mailbox were four letters. Tears filled my eyes as I read the warm words of my friends. I was so lonely. I passed by a cluster of birch trees, their branches reaching to the sky, holding the few golden leaves the wind had not blown away. I love birch trees. There is something so beautiful and clean about them. They stand out from the dark landscape. As I gazed upon these trees, their beauty overwhelmed me, and I felt the warmth of God's love sweep over me. Though my heart still hurt, it was strangely comforted. "From now on, whenever I see a birch tree, I will remember that God loves me," I said to myself through my tears. And to this day, every birch tree I see reminds me of His love.

In April 1994, Albert, our Liberian friend, had earned enough money to return to his homeland. Sadly we bid him goodbye, praying for his safety. We would miss this gentle and loyal friend who had been so much of our daily lives.

Within two weeks we hired a young physics teacher named Sasha Buts (pronounced "boots"). Sasha was about thirty years old, spoke excellent English, and knew much about computers. He had worked in Germany for a summer, so he had experienced the West and its business methods. He understood better than most Ukrainians how to accomplish tasks. Sasha had a German accent in his English that reminded me of Colonel Klink in the TV series *Hogan's Heroes.*

In August 1994, Sasha Buts became the recipient of an East German car, which his German friend drove to Ukraine to sell. He wanted $600 for the Lada station wagon, which seated five people squeezed tightly. After living in Ukraine for over a year, we were ready to have some dependable transportation of our own. Though we didn't have $600, we offered to buy the car through Sasha with installments of $100 per month plus the expenses to get the license tags, etc. and make any needed repairs.

Having a car would save us time. We also had many things to haul: 130 copies of the Berlioz *Requiem* to deliver to the rehearsal hall, for example. We could pick up large jars of juice and all the groceries we needed for a week. Heavy foods, such as big bags of potatoes, were difficult for Roger to carry since his shoulders were aching from bursitis, a new ailment.

In many ways, however, owning a car was a disaster from the beginning. Just the paperwork to *drive* the car took over a month. Every night we had to take it to a guarded lot and pay one dollar or risk having it stolen. Even during the day in front of our building, the car was vandalized, the mirrors and hubcaps now missing. We learned that the mirrors and windshield wipers had to be removed and locked inside the car every time we left it, even for a few minutes.

That fall Matthew's friend Blair, who had first accompanied us when we moved to Kiev, returned for a semester. He and Matthew rented an apartment just across the street from the guarded car lot. Since Blair had his driver's license, he was able to put the car away every night and bring it to our apartment in the morning. Blair had just graduated from high school and spent these few months singing in Roger's choir and tutoring Matthew in his eleventh grade home-school courses. Roger and I were no longer teaching at George McCammon's school, so there was no free tuition to continue Matthew's education there. With the business of concerts and our own church services to manage, we no longer could afford the time commitment at the school.

In October the choir and orchestra performed the Durufle *Requiem*, a wonderful concert. When we finally left the hall, it was quite late. The Lada, which suffered battery problems, now had very dim headlights. By law we were allowed only five passengers, but, as usual, Roger took as many as we could cram into the vehicle. Roger was driving, and I was in the front seat holding a lapful of flowers from the admirers at the concert. Squeezed into the back seat of the station wagon were Matthew, Sasha Sikorsky, and Sasha Buts, with Blair in the rear. Two other people were taken home as we made our way across the city.

Soon the dim headlights went out completely, and we were driving the dark streets without any light at all. My stress level rose as I strained my eyes, looking for pedestrians or policemen. Finally we came to the Paton Bridge, which crosses the Dnieper River to our neighborhood. The police were there, stopping many cars. *We'll never slip by this stop,* I thought. Sure enough, as we passed the checkpoint, we heard a whistle. Roger kept on driving. We all began yelling at him, "Stop! You have to stop!"

Roger stopped about fifty feet onto the bridge, causing the policemen to walk to him. The officer came up to Roger's window and demanded his papers. "Why didn't you stop?" he asked in Russian. Roger made some excuse. "How many in this car?" he asked again.

"Five people, of course." Roger answered. My stress level had reached the breaking point. He had not looked at the lights yet, but I knew that was coming.

The policeman walked to the rear of the car and saw Blair in the back. Angry, he returned to Roger and barked, "I thought you said there were *five* people."

"Yes, and one in the back," said Roger. We were in trouble.

I was so stressed and angry that I could stand the suspense no longer. "I am sick and tired of this stupid car!" I yelled as I got out and slammed the flimsy door. "I'll just walk home."

The policeman was so amazed at my behavior and my appearance, this lady in a pink chiffon dress with an armload of bouquets, screaming, that he said nothing and motioned Roger to drive on.

I was hot from my neck down, as I walked heavily on the bridge, alone. Soon I heard footsteps behind me. Matt and Blair had decided to accompany me so I would be safe. After three minutes I began to notice how cold it was on the river. Then I became aware how long I would have to walk in my high heels. The bridge spanned over a mile. Roger drove past me because he was not allowed to stop on the bridge and there was a fence between the walkway and the road. By the time I got home, I had a cold, stiff neck. Roger had had time to take the two Sashas home, park the car in the lot, and walk back to the apartment. From that time on, I hated the Lada. It was just one more unpredictable detour in my life.

It would seem that taking a taxi would be more reliable. Any car in Kiev can be a taxi. Most of the time you arrive at your destination as planned. One night after rehearsal Roger and I were offered a ride home by Volodya, an acquaintance, and his companion. We were driving through a deserted factory district that I didn't recognize. I wondered why he had taken this route. Then as we rounded a curve, we were stopped by two policemen. This is not unusual. One can expect a ten-minute delay, but this was taking so long. Both Volodya and the driver were talking with the policemen, and the conversation was intense. Then the policemen told us to get out of the car. This was an unusual development.

"I'm sorry," said Volodya, "but we have to go with these men to the police station. Just keep walking on this road and you will find your way home." As we stood there in shock, the four men got in the car, and a policeman drove the car away. Was the car stolen? Was it missing the license plate? We could not tell in the darkness. We walked through the fog in the direction Volodya had indicated. I had not felt so lost since the night we first arrived in Kiev. Then through the grayish-white mist, I saw a lighted sign, "Casino." For some reason the image felt familiar. Where were we?

Then it became clear. We had been on the other side of the underpass from the Tourist Hotel. This was the place we always arrived by metro to catch the bus to go home. One second we were lost, the next we were found. What a revelation! Roger and I boarded a waiting bus and arrived home forty minutes later, safe and sound.

These types of adventures were frustrating when they happened, but when I looked back on them, they were fun to share.

It was a few months later that Sasha Buts was driving the Lada and got sandwiched between two large trucks, totaling the car. Fortunately he was not hurt. We had completed our payments on the car and declared it a rental plan with no future.

I had never trusted Sasha Buts' driving. After riding with him the first time, I had sworn never to ride with him again. Children, dogs, and old women with canes flew from his path. I called it "Mr. Toad's Wild Ride." "Brake!" I cried. "Use the brake!"

I don't know whatever happened to the wrecked Lada or the license plate that we so eagerly and patiently processed. The heap of metal sat outside our apartment for a few weeks, and then it was hauled away.

Chapter 22
Precious Gifts

We were approaching our second Christmas in Ukraine when some special visitors arrived. Representing an anonymous foundation, they observed all of our activities. As one member said, "This is the most effective ministry I have witnessed in a long time." The power of music in the hearts of people, the message of that music reflecting God's glory and His Word, the development of the church, and the evidence of changed lives stirred their hearts. This resulted in three wonderful gifts that boosted our work a hundredfold. If we had been given three wishes by a genie, nothing could have served our work better. The Lord sent these people to provide our path for the future.

The first gift was a computer, one that could run Windows. Now we could format our own concert programs, church bulletins, and official letters with a professional appearance. Four months later it would be our channel for e-mail, saving time and money for our ministry. By 1995, communication to the USA was three dollars a minute. When our phone bills reached $500 a month, e-mail saved the day. The computer made this possible. It was a tool that lifted us to a new level of efficiency.

The second gift was money to buy a car. We knew we didn't want another Lada. Roger and the guys visited the car market. Hundreds of cars sat on the huge lot, each car occupied by an individual waiting for a buyer. Roger and the guys finally decided on a blue 1988 Volkswagen van that ran on diesel fuel. It had been used for hauling. There were two seats anchored in the front and a vinyl bench seat for three people unattached in the rear. We decided to have it remodeled with a removable seat so that we could haul orchestral instruments or people. It drove like a truck, but because it rode so high above the other cars, it appeared to be safer than the little Lada.

Again we started the process of obtaining a license tag. We put the title in the name of Sasha Sikorsky so that we could have a Ukrainian license plate instead of a foreign plate. This saved the driver from excessive stops by the police looking for bribes.

Even when the paperwork was finished and the fees were paid, we still had to wait a week to receive the license plates. Our lawyer had copied one digit wrong in Sasha Sikorsky's passport number, and some of the paperwork needed to be repeated.

There were times when we drove anyway. In the neighborhood that was OK, but one day Roger needed some spaghetti for the twenty choir members coming that night for dinner. He told Sasha Buts and me to go to the Italian dollar store, the only sure place to find spaghetti.

"Blair can drive you," he said.

"But it's on the other side of the river," I said. "What if we get stopped?"

"We've done all the paperwork, paid the fees, and have the receipts. The license plates are just a formality. Buts can translate for you if a policeman pulls you over," he said.

"But Blair doesn't have official papers to drive the van yet," I argued.

"Sasha Sikorsky must be in the car to be legal."

"It will be all right," Roger assured me.

No sooner had we driven onto the bridge than a policeman motioned us to stop. Sasha Buts and Blair stepped out of the van to talk to him, and Blair paid him three dollars. "Why such a big bribe?" I asked, as they told the tale to me. "Now he will look for us and want it every time."

"I know what to do the next time this happens," said Sasha Buts. "I will tell them I am Sasha Sikorsky and have forgotten my documents."

"No, Sasha. I don't like lying," I said. "We're all going to end up in jail."

Two miles later another policeman motioned our van to pull over. Sasha Buts got out and talked to the officer. Soon he was back in the van and we were on our way. "What happened?" I asked.

"I gave him two concert tickets, and he let us go," Sasha said. "He doesn't realize the tickets are for last month's concert."

"Sasha! Those tickets have Roger's name on them. Are you crazy?"

"I don't have tickets for next week's concert yet. If he shows up, I'll have some reserved for him," Sasha replied.

As we neared the neighborhood, Blair turned left across a ribbon of snow and was flagged down again by a policeman waiting there in a car. Sasha and Blair were asked to get into the police car while I waited in the van. After what seemed to be a very long time, they returned. Blair jumped into the driver's seat and started the engine. "That was my first traffic ticket," he said. "There was a solid line under that snow and I made an illegal left turn."

"But that wasn't our fault, if you can't see it and there is no sign," I defended him, forgetting that the policeman had not even noticed that our license plates were missing. "How much did he charge you?"

"In American money?" Blair glanced back at me with eyebrows raised. "Ten cents!"

I was really anxious to get to the store and get home. This whole experience was too tense. We proceeded down a busy boulevard with booths of goods for sale on each side. Even the fences were covered with clothing for sale. "This market has many police here because of the Mafia," Sasha said. We inched closer to the car in front of us to hide the fact that we had no license plates. There were many pedestrians crossing, and traffic was slow. My blood pressure was rising.

"OK, Sasha, how do we get to the Italian dollar store from here?" I asked.

"I don't know," Sasha answered casually.

"What? Well, *I* don't know this part of the neighborhood. I've only been to this store once, on foot with Roger from the other direction. I thought you knew where we were going."

"I thought we were going to Leviberezna market," answered Sasha.

"*Why* would we be going to Leviberezna if we are on *this* side of the river?" I asked sarcastically.

"I don't know," Sasha replied with a don't-blame-me attitude. "It's very *dangerous* to cross the river without a license plate."

"Argh!" I exploded. "Oh, well, let's hope we can find it from here. Turn right at the next light."

Two minutes later I saw a familiar landmark. Soon we were at the intersection where the Italian dollar store was. That wasn't its real name. It was one of the two food stores in the city where you could buy imported foods, however. The other was Swiss, and we called it the Swiss dollar store. Dollar stores accepted only dollars in payment for their products.

I quickly ran into the Italian store and purchased ten packages of spaghetti and six cans of tomatoes. Impulsively I grabbed a box of CoCo Puffs cereal for Blair. After all he had been through, he deserved a reward.

We took the long way home, going over a different bridge and through strange neighborhoods to avoid police. As we arrived safely home, I made a solemn vow to myself that I would not ride in the van until I saw the license plates firmly attached.

One week later the license plates were on the van, and we were legal. From that time on, I appreciated the convenience of having a large vehicle. We could now go shopping and load the van with goods instead of endless hours of riding the bus with overloaded arms. I could also take the laundry to the cleaners and not have to beg others for transportation.

On Sundays we not only transported the family and the preacher but also dishes and potato salad for sixty people. The potato salad fed the choir members who were attending both church and choir rehearsal. The three hour choir rehearsal immediately followed worship, and the singers needed to have some food .

Realizing that Blair would be returning to the States soon, Roger processed his own papers to be able to drive the van. Roger is a good driver, but after a month, he was frustrated with the police harassment. They stopped us for ridiculous reasons just to get a bribe. One time they said we did not stop at a crosswalk. The fact that "no one was in the crosswalk or even standing on the curb" did not matter. Then one day Roger parked with some other cars by a cathedral. Later driving down the road, he was stopped. "Where is your license plate?" asked the policeman.

"What? You mean my license plates are gone? Someone must have stolen them," Roger said in surprise.

Upon inspection Roger saw that the front license plate was missing. The back one was still intact. The policemen took Roger's driver's license. They knew something he did not yet know: The police had taken his front license plate for parking in an illegal area, even though there was no sign posted that said "No parking." Instead of putting a ticket on his windshield, they took the license plate—a condition one cannot ignore. Now it would take him hours at the police station to pay his fine and get both his license plate and driver's license back. These frustrations, plus the bad manners of fellow Ukrainian drivers on the road, took all the fun out of driving. Soon he was looking for another driver—a Ukrainian—who could handle this burden.

Matt had become friends with a young man named Andre Palukhin, a nineteen year old whose main ambition was to become Arnold Schwarzenegger. Andre was a body builder, street-smart and he was looking for a job. We took him on as a driver.

After Blair left, Andre became Matthew's best friend. They often exercised at the gym together and came over afterwards for supper.

Andre was a very good driver, safe in maneuvering the vehicle and calm in the most tense situations. He was familiar with the mechanics of cars. The first week he was working for us, he was waiting for his driving papers to be processed. He could drive on our side of the river without risk, so we were having him do local jobs. Then we faced an emergency.

Roger had a terribly severe migraine headache. It couldn't have occurred at a worse time. He was scheduled to drive the van to the Opera House to pick up the percussion and harp and deliver them to the Bieli Dome where he was rehearsing the orchestra in Copland's "Appalachian Spring" and some pieces by Gershwin. All morning he had tried to overcome it, soaking for hours in a hot tub of water. The time came to leave. As he was putting on his clothes, he stopped and said, "I just can't do this," with his face ashen gray. He sat down on the bed. "Someone will have to drive and conduct for me."

Calm on the outside but feeling inner panic, I thought, *This is impossible!* Not only was Andre without proper papers to drive the van, but I had no idea who could conduct the rehearsal, especially the very difficult Copland piece.

Edward Senko came to my mind. He was orchestral manager and teacher of conducting at the conservatory. Surely he would be at the rehearsal.

Andre and I climbed into the van and started toward the center of the city. "Let's not do anything to draw attention to ourselves," I said as I kept my eyes on the speedometer.

We were fifteen minutes late to the Opera House where we had to pick up the harp and the timpani for the rehearsal. We drove into the little lot lined with parked cars by the stage door. Fortunately there was a place right by the door, and Andre began backing into it.

Suddenly we heard a scraping sound from the tail end of the van. We had hit a fancy foreign car. Standing in the middle of the lot were two guys with thick necks and lots of jewelry. They turned at the sound of metal against metal, and the shorter one came running at us. He opened Andre's door, yelling, and punched Andre right in the face. Andre just sat there.

"Wait!" I yelled, "We'll take care of it. Don't worry!"

Andre pulled the van forward and we got out to look at the damage. The damage was minor. The red casing of the taillight was smashed, but the bulb was intact. There was a small scrape about two inches long and an inch wide next to it on the fender. The bumper, which was rubber, had no damage.

The short, Mafia-looking man was still yelling, saying it wasn't his car. The computerized black paint was going to be expensive. He said it would cost $100 to fix. I doubted that it would be so expensive, but he was definitely in control of our fate. I tried to give him my card, explaining who my husband was. If he would bring us the receipt of the repair, we would pay the bill. He shoved my card back into my face. He wanted the money now.

I had quite a few coupons with me from the ticket sales receipts for the concert. I counted out seven million coupons, which was about $10. Andre gave him four million more. Meanwhile I went inside the Opera Theater to find the orchestra players. When I came out, the man and his car were gone. He had taken the $65 and left. Andre looked devastated.

"Don't worry! It's all over now," I said. "I'm sorry he hurt you."

"I don't mind that," said Andre. "I just hated paying all that money."

We loaded the instruments and arrived at the Bieli Dome. The orchestra was seated, ready to begin. Edward was not there. What good was an orchestra rehearsal without a conductor?

I was running down the four flights of stairs to call Roger to say, "Now what do we do?" when I ran into Edward coming up. He agreed to conduct the rehearsal. I sat in the back of the hall, listening to the music, which he rehearsed slowly but accurately. Afterwards Andre and I returned the harp and percussion with no further incidents. When we finally arrived at the apartment, Roger was feeling much better. I was exhausted.

The next day Maynard and Nancy Sikes arrived for a visit. Maynard had come to record the choir and orchestra with his highly developed, personally constructed microphones. They resembled little jet planes and had the capacity to reproduce the choral and orchestra sound with exceptional authenticity. It was the first of several trips to Ukraine in which several CDs of the Kiev Symphony Orchestra and Chorus would be produced.

Andre soon received his driving papers and gave us great assistance as we carried the sound equipment to recording sessions, the Bibles and potato salad to church, the music to rehearsals, and instruments to the concert. He never had another accident with the van. And that van fulfilled a great purpose for us for a year and a half.

The biggest problem with our van was that it had a diesel engine and would not start in the cold temperatures of winter. We never did find a garage to house it. Eventually, after we moved to the center of the city, we sold the van and bought a smaller, but more economical, vehicle. Roger stopped driving entirely after Andre became our driver. The number of cars on the road and the stress involved in traffic was rapidly increasing. Eventually we gave up the small car as well and walked or took a taxi.

Though we found a new style of life without the van, the adventures and usefulness it provided in those early days living across the river will not be forgotten.

Chapter 23

Searching for a New Home

We were awarded money to purchase an apartment for the ministry. This was the third gift—a place of our own! The cost of renting apartments was skyrocketing. Our rent had doubled. It was only a matter of time until we could no longer afford the apartment. Perhaps we could choose a convenient location across the river, close to the center of the city, where we could be near our rehearsal hall and the offices with whom we were doing business.

We set a list of priorities for this new apartment. We wanted to have living space for us and office space for the choir and orchestra business. We also needed a large room for our Bible study—perhaps to accommodate forty people. We were so crowded with fourteen people in our small living room. Roger and I usually ended up on the floor for lack of space.

A lawyer in our neighborhood named Sergei said he would assist us in finding an apartment to buy. We knew the sizes of apartments in our neighborhood. There was no apartment large enough, and it was doubtful that we could find two adjacent apartments, both for sale, that could be connected.

We started looking toward the center of town in the government section called Pechersk. Many older, larger apartments were there, many with high ceilings. Most of the places we saw had two or three families living in them. Some were occupied by alcoholics. Laundry hung on clotheslines in every room; stacks of junk covered the floors; kitchens had no cupboards; toilets lacked toilet seats; walls had no paint or wallpaper. One had to have a good imagination to visualize what remodeling could do. Many apartments had big dogs that had to be tied while we surveyed the living quarters. The rooms smelled of dog and alcohol and dirt.

Finally we came to an apartment that was decent. It was occupied by one family and had three fairly large rooms with a kitchen and bath all opening onto one long corridor. Two of the rooms were quite nice with attractive wallpaper and had a balcony with a great view of the city. The building had a workout gym in the basement and was next to the Iranian embassy. The guardhouse on the street would be a great deterrent to thieves or other criminals. Though the apartment was not near a metro (about fifteen minutes' walk), it had a terrific view of the city from the top of the hill. We continued to look in that region, but nothing could beat this apartment. The apartment across the hall was also for sale. It might be possible to buy both and have a total of five rooms, two baths, and two kitchens. It still did not have the possibility for one very large room, but it seemed the best alternative. If we bought both apartments, we would have no money left over for remodeling, but the first apartment was decent enough without many changes.

Before we went home for our 1995 Christmas break, we had made the decision to buy these apartments. We gave Sasha Buts the power of attorney to close the deal as soon as possible.

Returning to Kiev in January, we found that nothing had happened. The owner had disappeared, and no one could contact him. For six weeks we waited for his response. Then one day we found out the truth: He was in jail! Buying his apartment was now impossible. We would have to start looking all over again.

We enlisted the aid of an agency called Diamond Realty, whose owner was a friend of one of our choir members. Having exhausted the Pechersk region, we began looking in the very center of the city. We saw some strange living conditions. One of the most memorable was what I called "The House of Doors." Inside the front door was a forty-foot hallway. To the left were doors to four rooms and the bath and toilet room. To the right were eight other doors.

Each opened onto a narrow closet with no shelves. At the end of the hall was a small kitchen. Four families lived in this apartment.

Because we still liked the neighborhood of the Pechersk apartment, we looked at one more unit on the hill descending to the main street of the city. The building looked pretty good; the hallway was not too dirty; and the front door of the apartment was tall and grand. A man in an undershirt answered the door. His hair was ruffled, and his breath smelled of vodka. He was very friendly, almost too friendly, as he tried to take my arm and talk into my face. He escorted us through some large rooms with high ceilings. I looked at the ceiling, thinking how this might be a nice apartment once it was remodeled. The floors were littered with vodka bottles and garbage. In one room a woman with dyed red hair was sitting at a small table with plates of food that gave an unappetizing smell. "Please sit down and eat with me," she said. No way!

The next room had one small bed in it. Under the brown blanket peeked a crop of blond hair. Soon a young head emerged, sleepily staring at us. "These people have come to see the apartment," said the man. The young woman yawned and crawled back under the blanket. It was past noon.

Then we entered the kitchen, which was quite large. The floor had black and white tiles, some of which had been pulled up, leaving holes to trip visitors. A stream of water flowed constantly from the kitchen sink.

We walked through the kitchen to another large room. There was a bath next door to this room. The dirt, the smell of the apartment, and the strange people were making me nauseated.

"Look!" said Roger. "We could put the bed here, and the dresser here . . . "

"Are you *crazy?*" I said.

I stumbled out of the room and across the broken floor of the kitchen. I had to get some fresh air. The man in the undershirt was following me, breathing on me. "Let me show you the rest of the apartment," he said, or something like that. Trying not to be rude, I told him in English that I needed to get outside.

I left the apartment and stood outside in the snow. The cold air and purity of the white surroundings helped to relieve me of my dizziness. How much longer would it be until we could find a decent place to live?

Lawyer Sergei was still making appointments for us, too. On one of them, I walked up to the door in the dark stairwell that had gray dirt an inch thick on everything. I felt sick to my stomach and said, "I'm sorry, I just can't do this!" and walked back to the car.

I quit looking for apartments, and Roger saw a few without me. One day he said, "Diamond Realty called. There is an apartment available just behind the Opera House." It was a cold, rainy morning, and I reluctantly went with Roger. We waited on a street corner in the rain for almost twenty minutes for the agent to arrive.

Finally our guide showed up and took us to the third floor. "First, I want you to see what is possible," he said, as we entered an apartment in the process of remodeling. It was an amazing place—light, large, and lovely—being transformed into a Western style home. Though their remodeling budget was much larger than ours, the floor plan showed many possibilities.

Then we saw the second floor apartment which was for sale. There was a small entrance hall with three doors. The light was dim and walls, unpainted. Behind the center door lived an older lady with two grown alcoholic sons. One was still in a bathrobe. The hall continued straight with two rooms to the left. The first room was littered with vodka bottles. The smell was suffocating. The mother's room was dirty and cluttered. Both of these rooms were fairly large with a wood floor and attractively shaped windows. The sons' room had a balcony that overlooked the street, and a large tree was visible from the window. At the end of the hall was a tall closet with no shelves and a smaller hallway to the right that proceeded to a despicable toilet room and a bathroom. Since neither had any lightbulbs, one could only imagine the filth by the stench. At the end of the hall was a small kitchen with an old sink that constantly ran water.

The other half of the apartment complex was occupied by a man, wife, and two children. Their section was cleaner and consisted of two rooms, a better kitchen, and a primitive bathroom. As we walked back onto the street, we played with the possibilities of remodeling. The mother's and alcoholic sons' rooms and hall could be combined into one large room. That would leave two other rooms, two kitchens, two baths. Yes, this had potential.

The agent told us that the apartment had just gone on the market, and the owners would sell if the closing could happen in two weeks. In Ukraine, this was practically impossible. Nothing happens that fast. We put a deposit on the flat that day, however, and started to work out the details.

The first problem was that one of the alcoholic sons could not find his ownership papers. Without those papers, no one could buy the apartment. Five days later, he found the papers in his bed.

We hired a lawyer that Sasha Buts knew. He met with us several times but only in restaurants or rooms without a telephone. "My father was minister of finance. I know the places that are bugged. We cannot even be near a telephone but that the KGB can listen to everything we say. They have that capability." Because the closing would be in dollars, which was illegal at that time, measures for secrecy had to be taken.

The real estate agents wanted to have the closing in their office. The thought of bringing $100,000 in cash to a public office was unthinkable. We finally convinced them to meet at Bank Aggio. The money could be received by wire and paid to the owners there.

We met at the bank with the apartment owners, the real estate agent, a private notary, and Sasha Buts as our translator in the vacant office of the president. The lawyer did not come. At the last minute he said he could not be present because the dollar transaction was illegal. The law stated that the apartment must be purchased in coupons. How ridiculous!

We counted out 100 dollar bills, dividing them into piles for each owner and the real estate agent. Each recipient counted their stack. Then the papers were signed, and the owners started stuffing the bills into their pockets.

"Are these people going out on the street alone with tens of thousands of dollars in their pockets?" we asked the real estate agent.

"Oh, yes," the man said nonchalantly.

"Isn't that dangerous? Can't you take them home by car?" Roger asked. The man agreed to assist them. As we left the bank, the two families started walking down the street to the metro. "Where's the car?" I asked Roger. Then the real estate motioned for his car to come alongside of them, and they crowded into it, safe at least for the moment.

We had an additional concern besides their safety. If they did not obtain another apartment with the money from this transaction, they could legally move back into the old apartment, living with us. "My worst nightmare," I told Roger, "is sharing my home with two alcoholic men in bathrobes."

Chapter 24

Stepping into Summer

By late spring, there were many new developments on the horizon. We hired an agent named Valeri to oversee the remodeling of the new apartment. The former owners had found other apartments and had purchased them. They now had sixty days to move out of the apartment we had purchased. They took every day of their allotment and more. We were halfway into June, and they had not removed all their belongings. We could not begin remodeling until the apartment was vacant. I was getting impatient. I so wanted to be living in the center of the city in a few months.

By June the McCammons had decided to move back to the United States. After their three years of dedicated service, God was closing the doors here on their school and church. Lifeline Ministries still maintained a health service clinic, but Kiev would seem different without George and Toni. They returned to Florida where George continued to pastor churches, Toni returned to teaching, and Matt continued college in America.

We had applied for a 501(c3) status as a new tax-exempt charity entitled Music Mission Kiev. This new organization with its board of directors and volunteer staff would make our work more efficient. We now had about two hundred contributors, and the monthly newsletter was attracting more interest in our music mission. The approval by the Internal Revenue Service of our new organization came the same month as George's departure from Kiev.

Time in Kiev was drawing to a close for our son Matthew. We had promised him that he could return to America for his senior year of high school. We were still not sure how we would find a home for him. Whom could we ask to take responsibility for a teenager who needed room, board, and transportation for an entire year? Orangewood Christian School, where he had attended two years ago, had offered a full scholarship, and he wanted to return there.

Matthew's two years in Ukraine had been independent study—the first year in George McCammon's school under the University of Nebraska correspondence program, the second year home schooling on his own at home. Matthew was looking forward to a real classroom again.

Meanwhile Roger and I were working on an ambitious project. We had received an invitation to bring a group of Ukrainian singers to the International Church Music Festival in Bern, Switzerland, the last week of June. Sergei the lawyer had been working for months on the paperwork to get thirty Ukrainians out of the country. Sergei Basarab and Sasha Buts were going along as translators. Sir David Willcocks of England would be conducting the Mozart *Requiem* in which several choirs from America would participate. We were bringing the tenor and alto soloists for the production. We were excited to bring an example of Ukrainian talent to an international arena to be heard. What hidden treasure!

In order to get Matthew back to America, we had to renew his Ukrainian visa. The renewal of visas was a constant struggle for Americans. Visas were issued for three months, and since it took a month for the process, one had to plan the next renewal as soon as he received the last one.

Matthew's visa was dangerously close to expiration. He wanted to go on a trip to Yalta with some friends from George's school before he left Ukraine. He needed to take his passport to show at the hotel there. His plan was to renew his visa at the airport when he returned. One could pay $50 there for a thirty-day visa.

When he returned from Yalta, however, the law had changed. Now no one could renew a visa at the airport anymore. Matthew's visa expired three days before he was scheduled to leave Ukraine. We had already purchased his airline ticket. We tried every way we knew to get Matthew's visa status cleared. No one would cooperate. To make matters more complicated, we were leaving with our thirty Ukrainians by train to Switzerland the day after Matthew was scheduled to fly to America.

Matthew never made that flight. Without a visa, one cannot leave the country. Even the American embassy could not force the Ukrainian government to allow Matthew to go home. In faith, Matthew moved his airline reservation to later in the week.

Roger was quite angry when he marched into the office of the Ovir (Department of Registration for Foreigners) on the morning we were scheduled to leave for Switzerland. Roger, with Matthew by his side, told his story to the director. Matthew had missed his flight to the United States. Even though he was willing to pay a fine, no one would help him. The director was unsympathetic. He did not care that Matthew was a minor or that his parents were leaving for Switzerland in two hours. Who would take care of Matthew until the situation could be resolved? And who would solve the problem?

The man looked at Matthew's passport and then at Roger's. Suddenly he rose from the table and said, "Just a minute!" Then he disappeared into another room. When he returned, he had stamped a new visa into Matthew's passport and did not even charge him a fine. Why?

Roger had had trouble renewing his visa a month before and had taken his passport and mine to the lawyer who was helping us close the contract on the apartment. This lawyer knew some people in high places and prevailed upon them to sign the visa approval. The signature in Roger's passport was that of a high official in the KGB. When the director saw his signature, there was no further delay on Matthew's visa. It was a "done deal."

I was waiting at the train station when Matthew and Roger arrived. We rejoiced at the news that Matthew had his visa and would be able to leave in two days. He would stay with Andre and his family until then. But the rejoicing soon turned to melancholy as I realized I was saying goodbye to our son. Matthew would not be returning to Kiev to live with us. And what a setting! Here we were in the same train station where we had first arrived on that dark, miserable night in 1992. The large statue of Lenin was gone, and daylight filled the room, but we stood at the doorway of our beginnings. Of all the changes we had experienced, this goodbye was the most difficult and the most significant. Life without Matthew would be different indeed. Though I was happy for Matt and his future in America, the core of our Ukrainian experience would be greatly altered.

As the call came to board our train, I left Matthew in the middle of the terminal, and I climbed the stone T-shaped stairway surrounded by our Ukrainian friends.

Two things helped cushion the blow of saying goodbye to Matthew. The Lord had brought a Christian woman friend into my life that month. Nancy Tyner and her husband Jim had moved to Kiev for a year. Though we had not met before, Nancy and I became instant friends. Jim was a retired engineer serving as a volunteer for the U.S. government to put cooperative ventures together between American companies and Ukrainian factories. I saw in Nancy a friend to talk to as I faced being an "empty nester" and changing neighborhoods. Our new apartment would be only a ten-minute walk to Nancy's apartment. Nancy and Jim were going to Estonia while we were in Switzerland, but we were planning to meet again when we both returned to Kiev.

Our trip to Switzerland occupied my mind and emotions as well. None of the group had ever been outside the Soviet Union before. Stanislav said Europe was nothing special. To him, no place could be better than Ukraine.

We traveled by train to the border of Hungary. From there our bus took us to Vienna where we were hosted by a church for two nights and presented a concert. The next day we drove into Switzerland. Stanislav kept looking out the window, not saying a word. He was seeing things he never thought possible. His spirit was overwhelmed by the beauty.

We stopped at roadside plazas and visited the bathrooms, which were spotlessly clean with white floor tile, white walls, and automatic hand dryers. Our Ukrainians took pictures of the toilets, to them a luxurious sight. Because food was so expensive, Roger and I bought food at a grocery store and then prepared sandwiches and salads in the back of the bouncing bus. Genna would take out his *bayon* (accordion), and they would sing Ukrainian folk songs as we traveled through the marvelous Rhone valley toward Switzerland.

Bern was a fascinating city of elegant buildings and modern transportation. The streets were clean and the sidewalks, neat and orderly. The city buses had steps under the doors that lowered to receive the passengers. "These buses are made for *people!*" the Ukrainians exclaimed.

Stanislav and Larisa were like two kids in a candy store. They went shopping together in every spare minute when they were not in rehearsals—not to buy, but to look. They were so exhilarated just to see all the beautiful things in the stores. The only purchases they made were two umbrellas for their daughters.

Our Ukrainian choral ensemble gave a concert for the rest of the festival participants. We won many friends and admirers there, some of whom kept in contact with us years afterward as supporters of our ministry. The Americans stayed in Swiss hotels. The Ukrainians stayed in local homes. It was a great experience for all, singing the Mozart *Requiem* under the expertise of Sir David Willcocks of England.

When our Hungarian bus departed on the morning after the concert, there were many tears shed as the Ukrainians left their host families. The Ukrainians left the festival week as changed people. As Anatoli Glavin, a tenor, expressed it, "I have no words!" Their hearts had been touched by the people, and their lives had been changed through the cultural experience of seeing a new world.

On the way home, I noticed how different Stanislav seemed. He was no longer grumpy and withdrawn but helpful and friendly to the others. We stopped at a rest area on a very hot afternoon. Everyone was thirsty and rushed with empty bottles to the pump in the middle of the park. Stanislav took over the pump, moving it up and down, serving others the refreshing water that poured out the spout and into their containers. He was laughing and joyful. He pumped the water for twenty minutes, until all the people had the water they needed. It was a sight to behold.

We crossed the border into Ukraine. As we waited at the train station in Chop for our train to Kiev, Igor, a baritone, said, "I feel like I have just returned to hell." The dreariness of the people and the unkempt condition of the station *were* depressing. Our group was grateful for the euphoric experience of the West, but they were sad, seeing the reality of their country with a new awareness. No longer could they believe that Ukraine was the most advanced country of Europe. To make matter worse, we traveled in third-class accommodations on the train—forty people to a car, sleeping on wooden shelves three levels high. It was hot and uncomfortable, but after eighteen hours we arrived in Kiev to the hugs of family members. Already I was missing Matthew as we walked away from the station and headed for our apartment across the river.

The next day we went to the new apartment where remodeling had already begun. The extraneous walls had been removed, and ten truckloads of debris had left the apartment. My hopes of a quick remodeling job were dashed as the job stretched months on end.

We traveled to America in August to raise funds for the mission and to see our relatives. Matthew had worked two months at Disney World and had saved some money. He was ready to begin school in two weeks, but he still had not found a place to live. "Matthew, if you have no place to live, you can always come back to Ukraine and finish your education there," I said. I knew it was better for him to remain in Florida, but who would take care of him?

On the last day before we left town, I received a phone call. "My name is Mrs. Frilen," a pleasant voice began. "Our children attend Orangewood Christian School, and we hear that you are looking for a home for Matthew so that he can stay in Florida and attend Orangewood next year. My husband and I usually have a foster child living with us, but our last child has left. We would welcome Matt into our family. We have a son his age."

We were thrilled. Again the Lord had provided for us—an eleventh-hour miracle. Matthew moved in with the Frilens for a year and finished high school with many wonderful experiences. His language requirement was transferred when a Russian teacher in the community told the school that his interview and Russian conversation with Matthew would be worthy of four years of "A."

Upon returning to Kiev, we saw that the remodeling was still at a plateau. The landlord of our present apartment was doubling our rent again, and we were anxious to move. I spent many afternoons at Nancy's house, walking with her around the city, becoming acquainted with the convenient shops and landmarks. Sometimes Roger and I would go to their place in the evening and play cards, enjoying warm fellowship with two Americans we loved dearly.

Summer was over, and our lives were in limbo between the old neighborhood and the new. The church was growing, however, and the concerts continued. Kiev was hearing for the first time Bach's *St. Matthew Passion* and *B Minor Mass* and a second presentation of the Poulenc *Gloria*. And every time we gave a concert, more visitors would come to our church. We carted potato salad in the van every week to feed the people.

We were plowing the field for the Lord, and our theme song was "Hold On."

Hold on to the plow that was Jesus Christ, and don't give up!

Chapter 25

From Worship to Widows

The little church we had begun with Sasha Sikorsky was
growing. We had a membership of thirty-five people with an
average attendance of fifty to sixty people. With the assistance of
Sergei the lawyer, the man who had attempted to close the deal on
the apartment adjacent to the Iranian embassy, we registered our
church with the government.

In September 1994, we had gathered fourteen people from the
church whom we thought had the greatest potential for leadership
and chose the name "Church of the Holy Trinity." The charter was
drawn up, and Church of the Holy Trinity became an official, independent Ukrainian church. Roger and I, as Americans, were not allowed to be members, though the committee designated us as invited teachers. Sasha Sikorsky continued to be the official pastor.

In November we started Sunday school classes for adults. Roger,
Matthew, Blair, and I taught separate classes with translators, and
Sasha Sikorsky taught a class as well. This gave us more time for
biblical instruction and discussion.

A year later the church was still growing in numbers and biblical understanding. We were also attracting many visitors from the
concerts. Sasha Sikorsky was talking about leaving Ukraine to live
in Japan for two years. He had applied for a special program that
would be paid by the Japanese government. If this happened, he
would leave Kiev in October 1996. It would be a great opportunity
for him.

Roger and Sasha had been sharing the preaching ministry of the church. Sasha would preach one Sunday; Roger would preach the next. Roger felt the need to be officially ordained as co-pastor. The people also wanted this, too. Therefore in November 1995, Rev. Vic Jackopsen, a Baptist pastor from England, and some visiting clergy from Switzerland performed an ordination service in which Roger was ordained as pastor.

It was one of the few times that Stanislav came to church with Larisa. Stanislav seemed very moved by the event and had tears in his eyes as he came to us afterwards. Though he had attended services about once a month, I still was not sure of his spiritual condition. He had heard the message of salvation many times. Had he embraced Christ?

One of Roger's first sermons after his ordination was "It Is More Blessed to Give than to Receive." The Church of the Holy Trinity is composed of many people who came directly out of atheism with little knowledge about the Bible. When Roger began with this statement, people laughed out loud. They thought it was a joke.

After the initial outburst, they listened as Roger explained the words of Christ. God is not pleased with our assemblies unless we are doing His work upon the earth. Part of that work is to care for the helpless, the orphans and the widows. This church should be helping the poor.

Help the poor? Everyone in the church is poor, but each one knew someone who was in greater need than they. From that day onward, the church collected an offering for the poor as part of the worship service.

The church began a feeding program for the elderly widows who had no family to help them. From the government pension office we received a list of twenty names that fit this category. We started buying food and delivering weekly packets to these women. It was not required that they come to church or even make a profession of faith to receive food. It was an act of kindness given in the name of Jesus

Christ. In an experiential act they were being taught about the grace of God—unearned, undeserved. Over the course of several months, some of the widows became believers, some started coming to church. All were grateful.

We wanted to take more than physical food, however. They needed spiritual food. Our church members delivered the food to their homes and showed them personal attention. We gave them Bibles. Many had no Bible. We bought them glasses so they could read again. We helped with medicine when they were sick. We loved these ladies, and they offered their love in return. Even before our apartment remodeling was completed, the first activity in the shell of the new home was the organization and distribution of food to the widows.

From 1996 to 1997, the number of widows grew from twenty to eighty-five. *Babuska* (elderly grandmother) banquets were organized where the widows were invited to Saturday afternoon dinners at the McMurrins' apartment. Special music was performed for their entertainment, and Roger offered a gospel message assisted by testimonies of faithful church members.

Though these *babushkas* were poor widows, many had prestigious backgrounds. Marianna Kosakevich's grandfather had been a favored military officer of Tzar Nicholas II. Her uncle played piano duets with Tchaikovsky. She studied ballet in Moscow. Her life was filled with tragedy. Her father was exiled to Siberia by Stalin for translating foreign documents. She was trapped in St. Petersburg during the World War II blockade and nearly starved to death. Though she was miraculously rescued, her health had suffered ever since that time. Now she was destitute in Kiev with an invalid daughter who cannot work and a pension of eighteen dollars a month.

Olya is an eighty-four-year-old woman who had been married and had five children. Two of her children had died from disease. Her son had threw himself under a train when his girlfriend married another young man. She has one remaining daughter, who stole her apartment to give to her granddaughter. Now she lives with this abusive daughter who says, "Why don't you hurry up and die so I don't have to take care of you!" She will not even allow

Olya in the kitchen when she is at home. Though the neighbors complain to the daughter about her treatment of the mother, it only makes things worse. Olya came to Church of the Holy Trinity and found friends there. She gladly attends Bible class, worship, and the fellowship dinner that follows every Sunday night. "You are my *real* family," she says with great joy.

Sophia is seventy-two years old and has no relatives. She grew up on a farm, but then Stalin seized their land. Her parents starved to death, forcing her to grow up in an orphanage. In her adult life she worked thirty years at the Opera Theater as a costumer. She created beautiful needlework and had given several pieces of her work to the McMurrins to show her appreciation for the food she receives. Because of very weak legs, she is unable to come to church. Not only is it a long walk from her home, but she also must climb four flights of stairs to the rehearsal room where the church meets. But she says, "I glorify God and ask Him to give health to all who help me."

Olga has lived all her life in Kiev and worked as a hydro-technical engineer. She is now seventy-seven years old, her back bent over almost ninety degrees. She supports her body on a cane. One night Roger and I were returning home from a concert. In the main metro station of the city, we spied Olga selling newspapers. She could hardly hold up the newspapers with her one hand. Recognizing her as a widow to whom we sent food, Roger took a twenty dollar bill from his pocket and handed it to her, saying, "Olga, you are working so hard and so late. Here's a little gift for you." She was embarrassed but quickly put the money out of sight and nodded her thanks. The next Sunday she arrived at church with an armload of lilacs cut from neighborhood bushes. She presented them to Roger as her way of saying, "Thank you for your loving gift." Since then Olga has been a regular attender at church and fellowship dinners. She is tougher than she looks. Contracting pneumonia, she was two weeks in the hospital, but she recovered and came back to church praising God. She joined our church a few weeks later.

There are many other stories—some suffered under Nazi occupation, some saw their entire families perish through accidents or disease or political persecution. They were teachers, doctors, nurses, geologists, artists, administrators, bookkeepers, and janitors. All their savings have been destroyed by inflation, and they have nothing but miserably small pensions of eighteen to twenty-four dollars a month. Many have found hope in the message of Christ and the fellowship of friends from His church. Even in their advanced ages, many have embraced Jesus as their Savior.

Valentina Yenichek, who supervises the distribution of food, says:

> The giving I see in this ministry is unlike anything I have seen in Ukraine. In the past people would give money to the poor as a tradition. Usually the giver would say to the beggar as he handed him the money, "Here is a gift for you; pray for me." This tradition continues even now. Today rich people who have received their money illegally will sometimes give to ease their consciences.
>
> There is a different spirit at the Church of the Holy Trinity, however. It is the spirit of joy and thanksgiving. I see it on the people's faces as I walk among them receiving their offerings. They know that God has given them His grace, and they show their love to Jesus with their money and their time as they provide for these dear widows.

The people of Church of the Holy Trinity have discovered an amazing truth: It is more blessed to give than to receive.

Chapter 26

It's a Palace

The long wait for the completion of our new apartment came to an end in February 1996. Roger and I were coming back to Kiev from the annual Music Mission Kiev board meeting in Orlando, Florida. Though there was some work to be finished in the apartment, it was still possible to move in. Sasha Sikorsky and his new bride, Julia, would live in our old apartment, finishing out the lease. While we had been gone, they had supervised the move of many of our belongings into the new home.

Sasha Sikorsky and Andre met us at the airport and drove us past our old apartment where we picked up the television and video player Sasha and Julia had been using. As the men went to carry the equipment, I stayed in the van, reminiscing in the starlight about our times in that neighborhood. After two and a half years, it really had become like home. Even the darkness, the barking of the dogs, the long building with tiny lights shining from thousands of windows seemed warmly familiar. So many memories had been planted here in this neighborhood—my total experience of life in Ukraine. What would our new neighborhood be like?

Soon we were in the center of the city, unloading the many pieces of luggage onto Lisenko Street in front of the little supermarket with the red awning. We carried the suitcases through the unlocked stairway up one flight of dirty and broken steps to the large wooden door of our new apartment. The stairway smelled of urine, either animal or human. With the absence of public restrooms in the city, both people and dogs had found this stairway a convenient relief station.

Entering the apartment, we found a few signs that it was being finished, but even with our coats on, the rooms were cold. To our left, major furniture pieces were stacked in the small, finished pink room. I had been told that only two rooms would be finished for living in this apartment, and I was prepared for this. I wasn't prepared for how cold it was inside, however. A draft of icy air was leaking between the old window frames, and the temperature in the warmest room was only forty-five degrees, even with the radiators working in every room.

The wooden doors had been nicely painted with a few brass doorknobs installed, and the parquet floor in the large room had been lacquered. As we walked through the large room toward the kitchen, I noticed the edge of the room had unfinished flooring where the hall had been. This area was covered with powdery dirt which we were tracking everywhere. Half of the floors were sealed with lacquer and half were unsealed. This was going to be a mess.

Turning into the short hall, I peered into the bathroom. We had the necessary fixtures, though there was no toilet seat as yet. The grout between the wall tiles had been painted pink, but the color was flaking off and would have to be redone. I had requested plain, inexpensive, white wall tile, but all Ukrainians argued with me about that. They said it would look like a hospital. Valeri's designers had suggested putting the wall tiles some distance apart and painting the grout *green*. I had disputed the green and finally settled on pink.

The kitchen was a pleasant surprise. The white cabinets were installed just as I had imagined them, with drawers that pulled perfectly; a tall, thin pantry; and a stainless steel sink. "Oh, this will be lovely!" I said. A white stove and refrigerator were yet to arrive, but for now the windowsill would serve as a proper refrigerator and even as a freezer between the double panes of glass. An old, brown stove in the back of the unfinished, second kitchen could serve in the meantime to heat water and do basic cooking. There were a few plates, four cups, a skillet and a pan, and enough silverware for our use. Unfortunately Valeri, our remodeler, had already installed brown linoleum in the gray, pink, and white kitchen. I never will understand Ukrainian color schemes, but at least the floor was not dust covered and could be kept clean with a mop.

Our oasis was the large bedroom in the middle of the apartment and our king-sized bed that we had slept on since 1970. The other Ukrainian bedroom shelves and cabinets were there too, though most of the contents were still at the old apartment. I found some sheets, but the mattress pad was missing, and the electric blanket no longer worked. I began to make the bed in the cold room. I knew, as I did that first night we spent in the Bereznikee apartment in 1993, "If I can only get the bed ready and sleep a little, things will look better in the morning."

Wearing as many layers as possible, covered with two quilts and the broken electric blanket, we tried to sleep with frosty noses. There was little sleep that night. We might as well have tried to sleep outside in the snow.

Dawn finally came. It was Saturday. The first order of business was to send Sasha Buts to buy two electric heaters. They were portable radiators, filled with oil, that rolled around the room on wheels. It added two dollars per day to our electric bill to use them, but it was worth it. As long as we kept the doors shut, the two heaters would warm the bedroom during the day to a comfortable temperature.

Roger went shopping for the widows' food with Andre and his brother. The widows had not been fed for two weeks because the van had broken down. Without Roger's persevering presence, the staff had given up and canceled food deliveries rather than solve the transportation problem.

The same thing was true of our telephone lines. Though we had two telephone lines in this apartment when we bought it, now we had none. The lines had been accidentally cut during the remodeling, and no arrangements were made to reserve and restore the lines. The phone company gave them to someone else, and it would now cost $1,000 per line to get new lines. Because of the high demand for phone lines, there was no guarantee we would have a phone line even if we came up with the money. Our application was sitting at the station unnoticed. Therefore we were sitting in a cold apartment with no communication to Kiev or America. Without a phone line, we had no faxes and no e-mail. This condition lasted for more than a month.

Meanwhile Valeri's workers started to remodel the stairwell and installed a lock and code on the outside door. When someone came to the apartment and did not know the code, they could not enter. Though there was a public telephone by the main entrance, they could not even phone us from there to ask for the code. It was disastrous.

Here we were, however, still in the first day of living in the new apartment. Sasha and Julia and some friends rented a van and brought four loads to the apartment that day—clothes, books, audio equipment, music, wall hangings, toiletries, bedding, food items, and various kitchen, office, and cleaning supplies. Somehow my broom and mop had disappeared during the move, but I did have dishwashing soap and toilet paper. Sasha Buts had thoughtfully bought me a toilet seat when he picked up the heaters. I could survive. I fixed lunch for everyone.

After the workers left, I washed the dishes in my new little kitchen. It is quite an unusual routine. First I light the gas pilot on the wall and hold the button down for sixteen seconds. Then I turn on the water, and the gas heater makes the sound of a roaring dragon. That's why this machine is called a "dragon." The water begins to get warmer then. Without this machine we have no hot water for bath or kitchen. It had to be turned on and used with care, for the vent tube was still unconnected to the vent in the wall. That made it necessary to leave the kitchen window open for ventilation, which lowered the temperature of the apartment even more. Though the building received only cold water, this machine guaranteed there would always be warm or hot water when we needed it.

This must be what the Medieval palaces were like—cold, drafty, with high ceilings and grand surroundings. Yet this apartment would become the gathering place of many phases of ministry for our people—from business office for more than ten employees, to concert receptions, from a distribution center for widows' food to banquets in their honor, from overnight houseguests to a gathering of seventy American women in their Christian fellowship meetings. There would be parties for youth, Sunday night suppers for the church every week, Bible studies, and family-life conferences. But now it was a big barn, mostly empty, with white walls and dusty floors.

A team of six women came the next morning to organize the widows' food baskets. Roger moved the fully extended dining room table that seated twelve people into our bedroom. This was another furniture piece we had shipped from America a year ago when our son Marc no longer needed it. The table became an assembly line for meat, potatoes, beets, bread, butter, apples, and cheese. Afterwards it became a banquet table, because Roger insisted fixing Sunday lunch for everyone. We found enough plates somehow, sharing the four cups between nine people.

"I just can't have people help us without feeding them," Roger said to me privately. I scraped and rinsed the dishes.

The ladies left for Sunday school, which began at 2:00 p.m. Sara Cocking, a Campus Crusade worker, would be teaching her last class on the Holy Spirit today. Next week I would resume my teaching of the class.

Roger would preach the sermon today, so he stayed behind to write it out, and Andre stayed with him. I put on my boots and black rabbit coat and went out to the snowy streets.

Chapter 27

A Slippery Path

Running a little late, I left the apartment alone, carrying a plastic bag of garbage and my Bible. I was going to be late to Sarah's Bible class. Our garbage dumpster is on the main street around the corner of our building. It feels strange to walk through crowds of people and carrying your garbage. I found the two dumpsters overflowing but managed to toss my bag onto the top. No one else but an American would bag her garbage.

Wow! I said to myself. *This is the first walk in my new neighborhood.* The frustrations of the apartment and its chaos faded away as I breathed the cold air. *I wish I had washed my hair before church. Oh, well, with this weather, I don't have to take off my hat.* I caught the trolley bus three blocks from the apartment, and arrived at the Bieli Dome twenty minutes late. After puffing my way up four flights of stairs, I walked into the large rehearsal room, where class was in progress.

I sat quietly at the back and noticed that many people were there, listening to Sarah's teaching and Sasha Sikorsky's translation. How I love these people, and my heart swelled with joy to see them. After the class, many came to greet me, and we exchanged hugs and expressions of friendship. Someone gave me a single pink carnation (a luxurious gift this time of year), and several offered to come and help with the apartment. Already a group of church women had spent hours cleaning two windows spotted with paint and years of dirt.

The worship service that followed was wonderful. A father and son played a viola duet; Roger preached a great sermon on salvation; and we were so happy singing the Russian hymns again. Being with our new believers and preaching God's Word—this is what it is all about. Now I really felt at home! There were about fifty-five people in the congregation, a few of them Americans. My friend Nancy Tyner invited me to join Jim and her for omelets at their apartment afterwards. I said I would come as soon as I greeted the choir at the rehearsal that followed.

This was the last Sunday night rehearsal for the choir. Roger and I had decided to eliminate rehearsals on Sunday nights and have church dinners and organizational meetings at our home instead. The choir would receive the same weekly pay for three rehearsals instead of four. After greeting the choir, I left the single apartment key with Roger and my new New International Study Bible with Andre to bring home later.

I left the building, carrying my purse and my pink carnation. The snow-covered ground lit up the darkness, and I caught the trolley bus across the street, which would take me one-third of the way to Nancy's. People on the bus glanced at my pink carnation, and at first I felt like hiding it, but then I thought, *Why not? It's an expression of Christian love from my friend.*

The bus came to a stop at the College of Communications, the same building where Roger had conducted that first rehearsal of the *Messiah* during our first trip in 1992. Stepping from the bus onto the snowy sidewalk, I walked along, twirling my pink carnation between my gloved fingers and feeling so joyful.

In a split second I was weightless. My feet slipped straight out in front of me, and the back of my head hit the icy snow with a hard and painful thud. Lying there in the cold snow, not expecting anyone to stop and help me, I could not move. Gradually I was aware of a burning sensation in my right arm that traveled from my elbow outward like a desert sun. *Oh, no,* I thought with a groan, *I've done it again—torn all those ligaments in my arm.* A year ago I had fallen at the St. Andrew's School and had my arm in a sling for a month. I asked myself the big question: Can I move my fingers? Yes!

Then I heard a Ukrainian woman's voice somewhere above me. I couldn't understand what she was saying, but I knew she was encouraging me to stand up. She kept saying it over and over again. Finally, with another groan, my body responded and I got to a sitting position. Now the arm was on fire. "I've hurt my arm," I told her before I realized she couldn't understand any of my English. She took my good arm and helped me to stand up. Still a little dizzy, I thanked her as she bent down and retrieved my black rabbit hat and handed it to me, saying sternly, "Be careful!" in Russian. Then she was gone. I never saw her face.

Alone again I checked to see if I had everything. Yes, my purse was still hanging around my neck the way I usually wear it, and my carnation, where was it? I was holding the broken stem in my hand, but the other half of the flower was gone. Bewildered, I dropped the broken stem and left both pieces there somewhere crushed between the soft, loose snow and the dangerous layer of ice beneath.

Longing for familiarity, I proceeded down the sidewalk only one block from our new apartment. From there it was a ten-minute walk to Nancy's. I staggered like a drunken person with my black rabbit coat gaping open and my right arm hanging limply at my side. I passed a casino brightly lit with red and white letters and a group of young thugs standing by their cars outside. Though I could almost see our building from there, I could not go home. I had given our only key to Roger. Even if I could get inside the apartment, I could not call for help. There was no telephone! No, somehow I had to get to Nancy's.

At the end of the block, was a taxi. *Surely he'll take me to Nancy's for a dollar,* I thought. (I had no coupons.) Yes, he would. I slumped into the back seat and watched the scenery fly by. When we reached St. Sophia's, a landmark I can pronounce that is close to the Tyners' apartment, I pleaded with him to drive two more blocks to the street I cannot pronounce where the Tyners live.

I paid the taxi and walked to the Tyners' door. Nancy answered the doorbell with a big smile. "Come in!" she said cheerily. I took off my hat and said, "Nancy, I seem to have had an accident. I fell and hurt my arm." She helped me off with my coat and said, "We'd better take a look at it." Since I couldn't pull up the sleeve of my turtleneck sweater, she got a large, warm man's shirt for me, and we removed the extraneous clothing to inspect the damage.

"Oh!" she gasped when she saw it. She helped me into the warm, teal-blue shirt and then said to Jim, who was in the kitchen preparing omelets, "Jim, you'd better come here."

"Zhee!" said Jim, wincing at what he saw.

"Well, what?" I asked, not being able to stretch my neck far enough to see.

"I'll get some ice," he said, and Nancy brought me a mirror. The elbow looked like it had swallowed a baseball, and the swelling was hard and tender. "Don't worry," I said, "I can still move my fingers, see? I did this a year ago. It's painful, but it will heal."

I lay on their couch for two hours with a bag of ice cubes under my elbow. At one point I was transported to the kitchen where I proved to them that I could efficiently eat with my left hand while resting the right arm on the ice bag on the table. By nine o'clock I knew Roger must be home, so I was ready to leave. The swelling had gone down somewhat. Jim and Nancy walked me up the hill to St. Sophia's and put me in a taxi for home. "If the lights aren't on in your apartment, have the driver bring you right back to our house," Jim said.

The lights were on. I rang the doorbell and could hear Roger's cheery voice as he approached the door. "Hi!" he said with his usual gusto. I showed him my elbow. Andre was there too.

"She needs to go to the trauma center tonight," Andre said, turning to Roger.

"But it's really much better," I argued, again clinging to the familiar. "We'll keep it on ice. If it's no better tomorrow morning, I'll have it X-rayed."

Since we had no refrigerator *or* ice, Andre went outside and filled two Zip-Lock bags with snow. One went into the bed on a little pillow for my arm, and the other went on the enclosed balcony where it would stay frozen until I needed it. I took two aspirin and went to bed with a heater to my left and packed ice and snow to my right.

It was evident the next morning that my recovery was going nowhere. The swelling had spread, and I could not lift my arm off the pillow without using my other hand to support it. The construction workers were back, lots of them, hanging the wallpaper borders I had brought back from America, installing the doorknobs, painting the grout pink again, and trying to fix the hot water heater on the wall. A leak had developed, which had ruined the ceiling of the *gastronome* downstairs, forcing it to close for two days.

I wanted to call the Lifeline clinic where I had gone before, but we had no phone. I couldn't remember the number, and I knew no one who *knew* the number. Sasha Buts was teaching at the Institute today, and Andre was buying slippers. (All residents and guests take off their shoes at the door and wear slippers inside the apartments.) Roger was making decisions with Valeri the remodeler, and Sasha Sikorsky was coming for lunch, which Roger was supposed to cook. So I just settled in my bed with my arm resting on the pillow, studying a chapter from my Russian language book. The lesson was entitled, "Must I Go to the Doctor's?"

Roger came in to tell me that Stanislav Pavlenko was coming with a car to take me to have my arm X-rayed. By this time, I was ready to go. When Stanislav arrived, Roger tied up my arm in a sling, and I left with him to go to the office of Valentina Surzhik, a choir member, who was also a doctor of radiology. Actually I had been there once with Roger when he had his shoulder X-rayed last year.

Stanislav couldn't get a car to stop for a taxi ride, so we walked the four blocks through icy snow. Though he could speak no English, Stanislav looked at me with sympathy and grasped my good left arm firmly but gently.

Valentina Surzhik met us in the entry hall with great expressions of concern and took us to the third floor where the arm was X-rayed in two positions. They were talking very fast in Russian as they looked at the results. She showed me the pictures and kept repeating in Russian, "Bad! Bad!" From what I could gather audibly and visually, the elbow was shattered. Three bones would need to be connected through surgery. I didn't want to believe it, but they convinced me my condition was serious—and now I was scared.

Valentina was calling different doctors and hospitals, saying that an American woman needed an operation. From her reaction on the phone, it seemed that no one was interested in taking care of an American in this situation. With each rejection, I was relieved. Valentina was my friend, and I didn't want to insult her, but I was horrified at the thought of having surgery in Ukraine.

I had heard horror stories from my friend and respected orthopedic surgeon Dr. Darrell Shea of Orlando, Florida. He had observed bone surgery in the Ukraine where doctors operated on three different patients in the same room, moving from patient to patient. Hip replacements with metal sockets in which "one size fits all" shocked him. He and other American doctors were amazed at the lack of sanitary conditions.

I asked Stanislav to go home and bring Roger here. Then I asked if I could lie down on one of the beds in the room. My knees were weak, and my whole body exhausted. Now I knew the reason for the extreme tiredness I had felt: My body was in trauma.

Roger arrived. He called Nancy Tyner and asked her to call someone who could contact Lifeline. Perhaps there was a Western surgeon available through the clinic. Nancy promised to hurry over to meet us after she made the phone call. Ten minutes later Lifeline called and talked with Valentina. From their conversation I gathered that we were to go by ambulance to a certain hospital and their resident doctor would meet us there. "Oh, good," I said. "Maybe he's American, or even if he's Ukrainian but Western-trained, that would be OK. He will probably speak English."

Valentina and Stanislav went outside to wait for Nancy while Roger and I were ushered down a back stairway to a little office where we filled out a form for the ambulance ride. Four people accompanied us to the hospital in this little red and white tin vehicle. The nurse sat with the driver in the front seat, and the doctor and forms clerk sat with their backs to them, facing us. Roger sat on the end of a small cot that was covered with a white sheet, and I sat in a vinyl-covered straight-backed chair with one arm. Fortunately it was on the left side so that my good arm could hold onto it as we traveled the bumpy streets. I had to scrunch down in my chair to see out the windows of this little "bug." I could recognize the streets. We were headed toward Bereznikee, our old neighborhood. Wait a minute! No, we were not going to cross the river. That meant we would be in Pechersk, the government section.

Our ride ended at the emergency entrance to the hospital, which in Ukraine means "the side door." The nurse led us down an austere hallway with cement floors. This looked more like a prison than a hospital. I did notice that the white Soviet wall tile I used in my kitchen and bath was everywhere. No wonder the decorator was shocked when I selected it!

We ended up in a drab room with a wooden desk in the center and a makeshift white vinyl couch with no back, where we were directed to sit. We watched a man on a gurney next to the desk as a nurse came in and drew some blood from his arm. She used no sanitary gloves. The nurse then wheeled the man out of the room.

Soon Nancy and Valentina arrived, and it was a joy to see them. The doctor arrived, a forty-year-old man with a thick, black mustache and a square build, wearing a white coat. He did not smile, and he spoke no English.

By all indications there was not going to be an American doctor here or a Lifeline representative. This place was as Soviet as Stalin. In fact this doctor resembled his picture. Just as I was about to say, "Let's get out of here," Sasha Buts arrived, breathless. He had been running to get here to be our translator. The doctor, after looking at the X-rays, said through Sasha, "Your elbow is shattered. You must have surgery today to connect the bones. If you do not have it today, you cannot have the operation for five days due to the swelling. It is advisable to do it as soon as possible. It will not get well on its own."

"How long will I need to be in the hospital for this surgery?" I asked. "Two weeks," was the reply. *Two weeks? In this atmosphere with no one speaking English?* I thought with a frown. *I know I need to learn Russian in a non-English speaking atmosphere, but this is not my choice for a classroom.* Then a nurse called the doctor out of the room.

"Well, what do you think?" Roger asked me.

"Roger," I whispered, leaning toward him, "I could *die* here."

"Do you want to go back to America?" he asked.

"Yes and no. I'm willing to stay if I can be convinced that this place is sanitary and the doctors are skilled in this type of surgery. But I know that I would be safer in America with Dr. Shea, a doctor I trust and with whom I can communicate. Yet there are so many hospital costs in America, and our deductible on our insurance is $2,000, plus the expensive airfare."

"Don't worry about the money," Roger said.

"Another problem is, because we fly Air Ukraine, I may not be able to get on a plane for five to seven days. You know how erratic their schedule is," I babbled on. "Delaying surgery may not be good either."

Nancy, who had remained quiet until now, took my good hand and said in her big-sister voice, "We need to pray for God's guidance." She led us in a beautiful prayer, asking the Lord to direct us and give us confirmation in our hearts with the right decision. Afterwards, through Sasha's translation, we questioned Valentina, whom we trusted as a Christian friend and a medical professional, about the reputation of this hospital and the doctors. She told us that this place—Hospital #12—was the top hospital for orthopedic surgery. It was associated with the medical college.

The doctor with the mustache came back with two younger doctors, both around thirty years old. They were the surgeon he had chosen for me and his associate.

"Well, what will it be?" Roger asked me.

"I guess I'll trust Valentina's knowledge of this place and these men. Even though I feel a little bit scared, I'll trust the Lord for the rest. Let's get it over with." Then I said with half a smile, "This will be a great page for the journal."

It was agreed. They would prepare immediately for the surgery. The fact that I had no health problems or allergies and that I had had nothing to eat or drink all day were good signs. They wrote on a piece of paper the kind of anesthetic Sasha should buy from the pharmacy. All patients must provide their own medicine.

The doctors left, and the nurse said to me through Sasha, "You must come and rest now." She motioned me to follow her. There was no wheelchair.

"Wait a minute," said Roger, and he leaned over and took my chin in his hands and prayed in my ear, "Lord, take care of my Diane. Give the doctors wisdom and bring her through this in good health. We trust in You. Amen."

Then I followed the nurse into the hall and there bid goodbye to Roger and Nancy. The nurse led me down a lonely hallway to two white wrought-iron gates. I passed through the gates, and she closed them behind me.

Chapter 28

Hospital #12

Silently I followed the nurse down another hall to the elevator, one large enough to transport hospital beds. We arrived on the orthopedic floor. The nurse brought me to a room with five beds, two feet apart, three beds on the left side and two beds and a sink on the right. There were no curtains between the beds, no chairs for guests, no bathroom, and no one who spoke English. I was assigned the empty bed beside the sink.

The bed was very narrow, with two parallel metal bars above it supported by a vertical bar on each end. The mattress was about two inches in thickness with a brown stain in the center. There were no sheets on the mattress. Another nurse came in with sheets, a pillow, and a blanket to make the bed while I stood leaning against the wall by the sink. She covered the mattress with a sheet that had holes in it, revealing the stain again. Then she put the blanket inside the top sheet like a pillowcase so that the blanket was visible through a diamond-shaped hole on the top. She threw a large feather pillow in a plain pillowcase onto the bed and motioned me to lie down. I climbed into the bed, carefully avoiding the metal bars and trying not to think of what the stain might be. Fortunately I was wearing thick, purple sweat pants and Nancy's extra large teal-blue flannel shirt for protection.

I slowly looked around the room to see my fellow inmates. It must have been visiting hours because family and friends were coming and going. In bed #1 was a blond woman with a cast on her leg. She used crutches to come to the sink. Her husband was with her, trying to help. In bed #2 was a shorter, jovial lady with a cast on her foot that was fastened to the end of the bed by traction. Two women friends were with her. They had brought apples, which they washed in the sink and shared with the other patients, leaving two apples on my bedside tray while I had my eyes closed. In bed #3 was a dark-haired lady who would have surgery on her leg that night. Her husband and children were there caring for her. In bed #4 was a lady who seemed very much alone. She had no visitors and had no visible cast that I could see. Though her face was sad, she seemed to be in a better state of recovery than the rest. I wanted to say something to her, but I felt so inadequate with the language, so tired from all the stress, and so bewildered with my situation that I just closed my eyes and tried to rest, wondering how soon the surgery would be. *I am in the middle of a Solzhenitsyn novel*, I thought. Years ago I had read his book *Cancer Ward*, which took place in a Soviet hospital, and now I was living it.

The Russian name for "hospital" is *"bol-NEET-sa,"* which means "house of pain." These patients seemed to be somewhat content in their stay here. Two weeks in this room was going to be an experience. I began to pray, thanking God that I was in this hospital and not in the African jungle or a Bosnian war hospital. Besides, I had Roger and Nancy and lots of friends in this city.

Roger and Nancy had gone back to the apartment to gather some items I would need: toiletries, clothes, and my Bible. I had to remove my jewelry and my watch upon admittance, so I had no idea what time it was, though it was now dark outside. Roger and Nancy had been able to visit my room briefly. Nancy had asked Roger before they left, "Couldn't we get her a private room, at least for after the surgery?" Then she turned to me and said, "I just hate to leave you here."

"Don't worry," I said, "I feel so much at peace. I know the Lord is with me. Everything is going to be all right."

A nurse in a baker's hat served supper to each patient: porridge and plain bread. I said my first Russian sentence to the nurse. "No food, no drink, the doctor says." She left it on my tray anyway.

I felt no temptation to eat this food. If I were going to be here for two weeks, at least I would have the advantage of losing some weight. No pork chops, no fried potatoes, and no vegetables would be served, such as I was accustomed to eating at home.

I heard Roger's voice in the hallway. He and Nancy had returned with a bag of necessities, including a roll of toilet paper. Sasha had brought the anesthetic from the drugstore and another translator for the evening shift. Irina Loktionova was there to assist us. I was so glad to see her. The doctors were almost ready for me, but they needed to know if I wanted a local anesthetic or a general anesthetic.

I didn't know what to do. My first response was "I don't want to feel any pain. I don't want to know anything. I just want to wake up and realize everything is finished." My decision was for general anesthetic.

Then the information came back that I would not have to stay two weeks: "If you have a general anesthetic, you must stay in the hospital for two days. If you have a local, you can leave in two hours and recuperate at home. Since you are an American, you have not been officially admitted to this hospital. In that case, you would have to pay the hospital over $1,000. But there is another way. You can have the surgery and leave and pay the doctors on the side."

"How much?" was our next question, to which the answer was, "The doctors cannot discuss this now. You pay after the surgery. It is up to you. If you wish, you can walk out of the hospital and pretend you never knew these doctors and pay nothing."

"Well," I said, "I guess I *could* have the local. I do want to go home soon, and it would be less risky than general anesthetic. Tell them I'll go for local." Irina went to find the doctors. Before she had been gone ten minutes, I said, "I just can't do it! I can't be awake while they're pushing wire into my bones. I can't stand the thought of a deep needle going into this painful, swollen arm. I must have the general. Please tell them." Nancy went to find Irina and the doctors.

Nancy and Irina came back together. The doctors had asked if Americans always change their minds this much. My doctor came in to look at my arm again and to say that the surgery would be soon. After he left, the other women in there gave the "thumbs up" sign, which meant he was a great doctor, the best in the hospital. I was in good hands. Then Irina told the ladies about our dilemma in choosing the type of anesthetic. There was a chaotic discussion among all the Ukrainian women, and they took a vote. They unanimously encouraged me to have a local like they had had. It was preferable.

Feeling better about the doctor and the situation, I said. "OK, tell them I now want the local."

"He's going to think we're crazy," Irina said as she left the room. The nurse came in and took my blood pressure and pulse. Then Irina came in and said, "They are already set up for general anesthetic."

So it was settled. The nurse came in again and gave me an injection to "relax" me, but I really felt more relaxed *before* the shot. Soon the nurse brought a wheelchair to the foot of my bed. At least I was not having to walk to the operating room. It was time to go.

I extricated myself from the metal bars above me and climbed into the wheelchair, noticing that there were no footrests. So, holding my feet off the ground, I was wheeled by the nurse into the dim hall followed by Roger, Nancy, and Irina. At the end of the long corridor, I said goodbye to my "family." The nurse turned the wheelchair backward and pulled me the rest of the way while I saw the familiar figures grow smaller until they faded into the darkness.

We turned a corner and followed another long, deserted corridor. I was beginning to wonder if I was going to some secret operating room. The temperature was suddenly very cold, and I wished I had a coat with me. I was still wearing the purple sweat pants and the flannel shirt that I had worn the past two days.

Finally we arrived at the doors of the operating room. They were locked. The nurse left me alone while she went in search of someone with a key. Then the doctors came with the nurse, and we went in together. I was told to take off my shirt, which I did. Then I was wheeled to the operating table. "Your head goes here," someone said in broken English. I climbed onto the table. Above me a circle of spotlights was turned on. I counted them—seven lights, but one bulb was out. The light gave warmth to the table as I lay there in my operating outfit: purple sweat pants and my white bra. They furnished no operating gowns.

I was wide awake. No one spoke English. There were three men and two women present. I glanced over to see the doctor with the black mustache, his mask not yet in place, but he was wearing rubber gloves. "At least they have gloves," I sighed. It must have been nine thirty at night. But there was a clock on the wall that read 11:21. I looked to my left, and a nurse was tightly tying a rubber tube around my good arm. I knew the needle would be next. I made a fist for her at her request and braced myself for the needle's long, slow insertion into my flesh. The bottle of solution above me bubbled and swirled. "I'm wide awake," I felt like saying. "Don't start yet. Nothing is numb. I'm too alert." Then a cool breeze blew across my face and back again. "Lord," I prayed, "Whatever happens, I leave myself in Your hands. If You want me to come home now, I'm ready." Then I relaxed and was transported to a different world.

I was in a very closed place like a coffin with colored lights inside. Yet I could breathe fresh, clean air. Every light was like a new pathway, and I could wander through the maze, exploring new paths like a video game. There were no monsters to fight, only the awareness of distant voices. It seemed to last about thirty minutes.

Then I felt pressure around my face, and a mask was being pressed against my chin, off and on. Two faces came into focus above me, and I could still feel the tug of the last stitches in my right arm. An X-ray was taken, and a wet cast was put around my arm. Then I was left alone in the operating room. I swiveled my head from side to side, trying to take in the details. The room was basically unfurnished except for the operating table, the lights, and the clock that now read 1:30. Then the two men returned.

With not a word, they motioned that I should climb onto the table that would transport me back to my room. It was over.

Meanwhile in the waiting room (the office where we had first met the doctors), Nancy, Roger, and Irina had been waiting for the past two hours. When Roger had watched me being pulled into the surgical wing in that wheelchair, Nancy said that the expression on his face showed that everything that mattered in his life was being taken down that hall.

Now, in the waiting room, the group of three was examining the human bone displays dangling on the wall and discussing which bone was which. Fifteen minutes into the operating time, the doctor came in and asked if I was allergic to Novocain. When Roger said no, he opened his desk drawer and took out a bottle of the stuff. Then he passed out some magazines to the family. He gave Nancy a fashion magazine, Irina a Russian magazine, and Roger, a "girlie" magazine. Then he went back to the operating room. "Who is taking care of Diane?" asked Nancy, sarcastically. "And how is it that he just keeps the medicine in his desk?" In America the nurse provides all the supplies from the medical cabinet ahead of time.

The minutes dragged into hours. They kept looking down the deserted corridor, but there was no sign of me. No one gave them any report during that time. Why was this "twenty-minute" operation taking so long? Finally, Irina saw a bed on wheels approaching. It was me, covered with a white sheet, my white face showing. Now conscious, I was able to talk with them, but in a groggy manner. They escorted me back to Ward #510, where one of the other patients had just arrived with a new cast on her leg, all the way over her hip.

The doctor told Roger that I could leave in three hours (2:00 A.M.), and that he would drive us home in his car. I wouldn't be able to have any pain medicine until then. Irina and Nancy left to catch the last metro home. They knew that I was through the worst of it now. Roger remained with me as the ladies slept. A table lamp under the sink provided a little bit of light. Roger helped me put on the flannel shirt. I was grateful that it was so big and comfortable.

An hour later the doctor reported that he had to do another surgery, so it was better that Roger leave and come back at 7:00 A.M. Roger took the packet of pain pills, opened one of the four foil covers, and left it on the bedside table with a glass of mineral water and a wet cotton ball that he had used to moisten my dry lips. "Take this in the night when you need it," Roger said. I didn't know what anesthetic I had had. I didn't know what medication was in the little foil packets. I just knew that I was tired and needed to lie still. There were no side guards on the narrow bed, and I feared I would roll onto the cement floor if I tried to turn over.

After Roger left, I slept restlessly. I was aware of someone snoring on the other side of the room. When I woke up, my arm was hurting, and I needed that pill. No nurse had come into the room since the surgery. In fact, there was no button to call a nurse in case of emergency. No one had taken my blood pressure, pulse, or temperature. Again I was alone. Should I take the pill? What time was it? I had given Roger my watch and jewelry when I was admitted. If I didn't know what time I took this pill, how would I know how soon I could take the next one?

I got out of bed, walked past my neighbor's bed and pulled back the curtain at the window. The sky was still black. *No, I won't take the pill until I can be certain of the time,* I told myself. I climbed back into bed grasping the metal bar with my left hand to maneuver. I lay there waiting. Finally the lady across the room stopped snoring and sat up.

"What time is it?" I asked her in Russian.

"Six o'clock" she said.

Finally, I thought. I took the pill and went to sleep.

I was awakened by Roger's entrance into the room at 7:00 A.M. It was time to go home. I was glad that I had taken the pain pill because now I had a lot of moving to do. Getting up, I walked across the hall to the bathroom, carrying my own toilet paper. The toilet had no seat on it, no top on the tank, and no way to flush it. It just kept running water slowly. It was the only toilet for the entire floor of patients.

Outside, the doctor and Roger were waiting for me. They helped me into my black rabbit coat, and we walked to the emergency entrance where the doctor's car was waiting. It was cold outside, and I felt like I was escaping from a prison with the secret help of one of the guards.

Soon we were driving along the streets of Kiev, arriving at last in front of the entrance to our building. The doctor, Peter Volk, who now was quite pleasant, bravely spoke a little English and came into the apartment with us. Roger thanked him and gave him $300 for which he was very grateful. This was equal to six months salary from the government. He said he would come back to check on me tomorrow. Roger had my medicine (antibiotics and pain pills), and he would be my nurse from now on. I lay down in my rabbit coat on the king-sized bed. It had never felt so good.

I faithfully took my medicine and rested. Roger cooked me a healthy breakfast. The workers were around all day, but our room, though surrounded by the unfinished rooms, was sufficiently private with two lockable doors. Roger had not slept at all the night before because he had no alarm clock and thought he would be late to the hospital. He took a nap, too. With no telephone at the apartment, there was little demand to get up.

During the next few weeks, the doctor made house calls to the apartment to check on my progress. Three months later, I had the wire taken out of my arm at the same hospital, this time with local anesthetic. Later, American doctors told me it was a miraculous healing. I had the full use of my arm, and, though it was somewhat weaker than before, I came to full recovery.

Chapter 29

Tour to America

After three years of giving concerts in Kiev, we began making plans for an American tour. We wanted to bring members of our choir and orchestra to America for five weeks. Roger had planned this for a long time: to give Americans a chance to hear this tremendous talent and to allow Ukrainians to see how hard work and determination can make dreams come true in the American culture. We would stay in the homes of American church families and perform in churches, colleges, and concert halls.

At first we sought help through various foundations for our tour project, but our organization Music Mission Kiev was either "too religious" for those interested in culture or "too secular" for those interested in religious objectives. We slipped through the cracks. Not all of our performers were Christians, though 80 percent of the choir were new believers. Even so, we were bringing the "mission field" to the churches. The purpose statement of Music Mission Kiev was not only "to present the Western classic masterpieces that had been forbidden under Communism to the nation of Ukraine" but also "to proclaim the gospel of Jesus Christ to and through Ukrainian musicians to the world." The latter shortchanged our opportunities to capture the interest of the cultural foundations. Therefore we stepped out in faith to organize a tour with a budget of $200,000 with the support of sponsors and local concert presenters.

From the time of my surgery at Hospital #12 until August (the month our tour was to begin), we gathered and presented information for the American Immigration and Naturalization Service (INS). This included passport information for 113 Ukrainians, articles about our musical group, programs of our concerts, reviews, and endorsements.

Meanwhile we processed all the Ukrainian passports for exit stamps (permission to leave the country). We hired a Ukrainian lawyer full-time to come to our apartment to work on all the documentation. Roger went to America in April and talked to all the host churches by telephone to finalize arrangements. We wrote biographical stories of each choir member and sent information ahead to the concert hosts so that the host families would know something about their guests. We worked every day from the time we awoke until late evening on this project.

Finally it was time to pay the airline Aeroflot for the plane tickets, totaling over $100,000. For this we had collected 50 percent of the $3,500 concert fees from most of the churches in America and borrowed some money from our board members. We still had not received the official letter from the INS, which would approve our visas, but we were told that since the American Federation of Musicians had approved our application, approval from the INS was a rubber stamp. Not to worry! We had filled out so many papers and sent so much documentation that surely there would be no problem. We purchased tickets for 113 people.

That night we received a fax from the INS that stated we had *not* been approved. They claimed we had not proven that we were "culturally unique." There was no phone number we could call. The fax had been received from our lawyer in America who had received the INS notice by mail. The INS is completely unreachable except for a post office box. We would have to apply all over again by surface mail. With just two weeks until the tour, this was impossible. We were doomed! The non-refundable tickets were in our hands, but we would not be admitted on American soil.

That night, completely exhausted, I lay in bed praying: "Lord, this is Your mission. If we truly cannot get into America with our people, we have no choice but to sell the apartment and all the assets in Kiev, pay back the money to the individuals and organizations, and give up our mission here. I'm willing to do that if that is Your will. But if You want this mission to continue, I know You will show us a way." I went to sleep fully surrendered to the fact that it was out of my control.

The next morning Roger and I went to the American embassy. We walked into the consulate's office and sat down. Roger and the consulate talked at length about the problem with no resolution. I had not said a word. Finally I said quietly, "Mr. Friedman, isn't there something that can be done . . . *anything* to resolve this problem?"

Mr. Friedman thought and mused, "Well, I didn't know that you were paying your musicians only two dollars a day for their services. I had assumed that it would be a professional scale. All right, if you write me a letter about the following topics, and if I *like* the letter, I may find a way to give you tourist-business visas."

That was all we needed—a hint of hope. We left the office, wrote the letter that day, hand delivered it, and three days later received a reply. Yes, we could buy tourist-business visas for fifty dollars each. The expense was more than $5,000, but it was better than losing everything. The approval went with the stipulation that each person would have to appear and be examined by the embassy. Later even that requirement was waived. "Just bring the box of passports," we were told.

Roger and I were leaving Kiev a week before the tour to prepare for the arrival of the group (buses at the airport, rented van for the instruments, rented instruments ready for the first concert, etc.). Our departure was scheduled for Sunday. We had taken the passports to the embassy the preceding Tuesday. By Friday morning we had not received the visas yet. "Come this afternoon," we were told. At 4:55 P.M. that day we had the visas, and the bill was paid. We were the last customers out of the embassy as it closed for the weekend. This tour was on!

The choir traveled through Moscow, where they stayed overnight and arrived in New York the following day. With the rented harp and timpani and buses ready, Roger met them at the JFK International airport, and they drove to Elizabeth, New Jersey, where they presented their first concert.

We traveled in two fifty-five passenger air-conditioned buses for five weeks. One of the Ukrainians drove a fifteen passenger van that carried the larger instruments: timpani, contrabass, and two cellos. The group included sixty singers, thirty-five orchestra members, five soloists, and a staff of twelve to translate, handle the sale of recordings, and organize the people. We even took a member of the Ukrainian government with us, Mr. Timochenko, administrator of the Conservatory. He gave an official greeting at concerts, representing Ukrainian-American cooperation.

The concert halls, sanctuaries, and college auditoriums were full or overflowing at almost every concert. In Jefferson, North Carolina, people were standing in line around the block to enter the gymnasium where we performed. In Orlando, chairs lined every aisle with all seats full, and people were turned away. In Jacksonville, Florida, people not only filled every chair but also stood in a solid line against the walls of the auditorium and sat on the floor down front.

Something extraordinary happened when these musicians performed. The audiences were captivated. From the opening processional of "O Come All Ye Faithful" to the finale of "God Bless America," the atmosphere was electric. Composers rarely heard in American concerts, such as the Rachmaninoff "Vespers," Leontovich, and festive Ukrainian folk music, stirred great enthusiasm. The concerts were "more than music." We still cannot explain it in words. Was it that these Ukrainians had been enemies of America under Communism but now were coming as friends, many of whom were now Christians? Was it that their musical talent was extraordinary? It was a quality that was often described by the words "splendor" and "another world." Night after night the same concert was performed, sometimes ten nights in a row, but the presentation was always fresh, as if it were the first time. Ukrainians demonstrated not only their talent but also their endurance as they executed great performances in a grueling schedule. Because we were not yet well known, we had to give many concerts to pay the expenses of such a tour. But the people responded so enthusiastically that at the end of the two-and-one-half-hour concert, they did not want the evening to end. Many stampeded the tables where recordings were for sale. By the middle of the tour, we had sold all three thousand musical recordings and had to reorder more.

Following each concert, the Ukrainians went to the host homes in pairs. Often they were in a home for only one night. Somehow, even with the language barrier, they became close friends with the people. The next morning everyone was crying at their departure, including the Americans. We would gather outside the bus and sing a farewell song for our hosts, "Prayer of Ukraine," which is an anthem that asks God's blessing on the country of Ukraine. We left each town with a packed lunch for the day and usually stopped at a rest area on the interstate that had picnic tables and restrooms. The Ukrainians were happy being in the American outdoors, and it was always a challenge to get them back on the bus for another four hours of travel.

The American people were so generous to our Ukrainians. They received everything from used clothing to roller blade skates. Some hosts took their guests to Wal-Mart and gave them money for shopping. These twenty-four-hour stores saw Ukrainians shopping at 3:00 A.M. Upon first entering a Wal-Mart, one Ukrainian asked her host, "Is this store for rich people?" "No," the host answered, "just normal people." "Unbelievable!" replied the Ukrainian. The great shock experience of the American culture was the supermarket, with so much food available. It brought tears to Ukrainian eyes. With the generous gifts, the suitcases were soon bulging, and we couldn't get the luggage compartment doors closed on the bus.

During the five weeks we were giving concerts, we shipped three loads of accumulated goods back to Kiev, each one weighing two thousand pounds. On a shipping day every room in the local church would be full of Ukrainians packing their articles into paper grocery sacks, taping them with mailing tape, and writing their names on the sacks with indelible marker. Then the grocery sacks were deposited in big shipping boxes that eventually made their way to a port and traveled by ship for six weeks to Ukraine.

What was the Ukrainian response to seeing and living in America?

They were amazed by the road systems and the number of cars and private homes. They admired the architecture of the cities, the cleanliness of the streets, and the beauty and size of the American churches and homes. They found that churches, homes, and even transportation are designed for the needs of people. They admired the warmth of the Christian family and the love displayed to children and guests.

Diana Milevska, the blonde soprano who had attended our Bible study, said, "People in American know how to work and how to rest. I will never forget meeting with Christian families, which strengthened my belief. I now want to work hard and help our people."

Music Helen (Helen Sedih) commented on the marvelous care the Americans gave to the Ukrainians. "I miss communicating with our papas and mamas who took care of us the whole time and kept us like small children. That was great!"

True, the Ukrainians who had no money and little experience of being outside their own country were cared for like children, even though they were intelligent adults. Without speaking English in America, many were quite helpless.

Mila, my soprano buddy from 1992, who sang "Summertime" by Gershwin in the concerts, commented, "I met many believers in America, and I know God has blessed them. I learned that even if people are not wealthy, their life can still be very rich spiritually. I would like to have this same spirit."

Valentina Yenichek, the little blonde who was baptized in our church and runs the widows' ministry, said, "I remember all my new American friends and miss their smiles. My belief in Jesus Christ grew stronger, and I have hope that all people in the world can live in peace because of the good news of Jesus Christ that we carry in joy and love.

Sasha Donskoy, the atheistic Jew who came to faith in Jesus in our Bible study and now serves as church treasurer and administrator, says, "I liked the fact that all citizens rely on themselves and on God, but not on the State. And that freedom is written in the law and supported by the attitude of the government. Since the tour, I am dedicated to helping Roger build a church in Kiev for the future of my family and my community."

As impressed as the Ukrainians were at American life, the Americans discovered that the Ukrainians had made a lasting impression on them, too.

Says Robin Henn of Palm City, Florida, "I miss my new friends very much. I told them that they have melted my heart. I never would let myself get close to people or was really concerned about other people's needs. People told me I had a heart of stone. God has worked in my heart in a mysterious way, and it was through them. I am a different person today."

President Bill Hurt of Montreat College wrote in an editorial to his readers, "I am still basking in the warm glow from the visit of the Kiev Symphonic Orchestra and Chorus. Somehow, the event magically became something much more than a performance, more than the meeting and making of new friends, more than even an international experience. We became a communion of hearts. It was people, faith, the wonder of Ukrainians at all things American, and, of course, music. As one faculty member commented, 'I came expecting a great evening of music but was not prepared for what was a life-changing experience.'"

Sermons were preached about the experience in churches following the tour. This excerpt comes from North Carolina:

> I stood outside our house very early Thursday morning, drinking a cup of coffee. My wife and I hadn't slept much that night—up until 2:00 A.M., packing lunches for Christopher and Victor—waiting for their laundry to finish—so they might have clean clothes for the next several days. We were still talking past midnight, sharing stories of our lives and our living—sharing pictures of our families, cultural differences, economic situations, political policies, the stuff of every society . . . . My coffee

doesn't taste quite so good on Thursday morning as I come face to face with these two Christian men: One African black who speaks English—so pleasant, so friendly, a thirty-two-year-old man studying international law in Kiev, singing in the choir—one white, aging man who speaks no English but communicates with his eyes a body language of love and appreciation . . . those eyes, so warm, so loving. These two strangers from a far-away place are poor, extremely poor by the world's standards, but rich, exceeding rich, in love.

A person from Fort Lauderdale wrote to us an impression of the concert:

The music was the best I have heard since we moved more than two thousand miles from the Metropolitan Opera. But the commentary offered between numbers, the happy expressions on the faces, the evident joy gave testimony to the effect an evangelical witness to Christ can have in a troubled world. These Ukrainian believers just let their light shine, and it was wonderful to behold.

Finally from Palm City, Florida, near Palm Beach:

We felt it was an experience of just what God wanted the world to be—people who were different not only in language but in upbringing . . . meeting and accepting one another . . . understanding that we *are* all alike, laughing, crying, loving, and praying together—it was wonderful!

By the end of the five weeks, having traveled over ten thousand miles in the buses and given thirty-five concerts, we were ready to bring the experience to a close. Our last concert was at Riverside Church in New York City. The next day we would say goodbye to the whole group as we put them on the plane for Moscow and then Kiev. Roger and I would need a two-week rest before we returned to Ukraine.

That night after the concert we drove through New York City toward Times Square. "They must get out and see the lights," Roger said.

"No," I objected. "It's almost midnight, and someone will get lost."

Roger, however, had the buses stop and he led the 110 Ukrainians into the streets of New York. I stayed on the bus. The buses moved to the designated spot on 42nd Street where we were to meet. Forty minutes later Roger returned with the crowd. We counted heads, and, sure enough, two ladies were missing. Roger and one other choir member went to look for them. We waited another hour until the ladies returned with Roger. They had stopped to shop and got lost in the crowd.

It was 2:00 A.M. when we pulled into the motel in New Jersey. I gave Roger the list of people and said, "Good luck!" as he supervised the unloading of the luggage and the assignment of 110 Ukrainians to motel rooms. Weary almost to the point of tears, I stayed in the bus imagining the chaos within.

After fifteen minutes Roger came to the bus and said, "Everyone has departed for their rooms. Are you ready to find our room now?"

"How did you do that so quickly?" I asked, realizing how time consuming room assignments can be.

"I just said, 'The first four people who come to me as a group get the first key.'" And the tired travelers were quick to organize themselves with very little noise or confusion.

The next morning we met in the motel restaurant where a breakfast buffet was served. "All You Can Eat" was a dangerous slogan for the restaurant owners. Our musicians emptied the large pans of bacon, eggs, pancakes, biscuits, pitchers of juice, and bowls of fresh fruit. They have amazing appetites. Everyone was so happy. Their suitcases were packed with souvenirs for family and friends. They were so anxious to be with their loved ones again.

We gathered by the buses and gave gifts to our drivers with sincere words of appreciation. It was time to leave. We boarded the buses and counted heads. Five people were missing. Inspection of the motel showed they were not there. Finally one of the choir members said, "I think I saw some people heading for the discount store several blocks away."

I was upset. This day would be quite complicated. We not only had to get to the airport, which was at least two hours' drive from the motel, but we also had to go into downtown New York City to a Ukrainian souvenir shop. Why?

Some of the tour members had purchased souvenirs in Ukraine to sell for personal profit at our concerts. This was against our rules because we were already selling compact discs and cassette tapes to benefit the entire group. Several times we had chased after the renegade musicians selling on the side. Despite repeated warnings, they continued to sell wooden trinkets and tapes of their other Ukrainian choirs to the concertgoers like ticket scalpers as they exited the hall.

When we confronted them about our rules, they said, "We invested a lot of our own money in these souvenirs. It was not clear that we were not supposed to sell. Our other choirs do this on their tours."

Finally we reached a compromise. We called a souvenir shop in the Ukrainian section of New York City, and the owner said he would buy the souvenirs from our tour group. The three men who had a significant number of souvenirs were permitted to unload their trinkets at the store on the last day of the tour. Of course, there were others who had a few extra souvenirs in their suitcases. They had been giving them to their overnight hosts, and they had a few extra. Roger decided that only these three men would be allowed off the bus to make the business transaction with the owner of the store.

Here we were, however, still in the parking lot of the motel with five Ukrainians shopping, unaware of our complicated schedule. Roger had the bus drive to the discount store, and he ran inside to find his people. A few minutes later he came out with two of them. They jumped on the bus, but one man was begging Roger to wait. His wife was still in the store with one of our translators.

"No," said Roger, "we are leaving *now!* They can take a taxi to the airport. It's their decision. We cannot miss the plane."

As we drove out of the parking lot, there was a low moan from several of the musicians. "A taxi ride from here will be more than $100," one said. "They do not have money." We looked back, but still there was no sign of the two wanderers.

After two blocks, Roger told the bus driver to pull to the side of the road. Then he went to the van that was carrying the instruments and pushed the occupants out. He got behind the steering wheel and drove like a maniac toward the discount store.

Fifteen minutes later we saw the van with Roger and the other two lost sheep inside. Everyone cheered. Roger escorted them onto the bus. They were both visibly shaken. They had wanted to pick up some last minute items, but surrounded by so many aisles of merchandise, they had lost track of the time. One lady had been hysterical when she came out of the store and saw the group was gone. Rescued by Roger, they promised never to do that again.

Now came the problem of the souvenirs. We drove toward the center of New York City, already behind schedule. As we approached the neighborhood, Roger said on the microphone, "No one gets off the bus, except the three men I have designated. No excuses." Then he told me, "You must not let anyone leave."

On my guard, I saw the first unauthorized person come forward to leave the bus. "No one leaves this bus," I said in my teacher tone. It took a long stare and a hand locked across the aisle to show them I meant business. I was guarding Pandora's box, and if anyone scattered, it was "all over."

Roger came back to give us an update. "This is taking longer than I thought," he said.

"Why don't you take the van and let us go on to the airport? We'll meet you there. Then if you have trouble, we at least will have all but three people checked in." I said.

"Good idea," Roger said. So the occupants of the van came onto the buses, and Roger and the three men stayed behind.

Feeling safe again, my security was short-lived when the buses made a wrong turn and ended up circling through China Town. I kept looking at my watch, praying and sighing deeply.

Finally we got onto the bridge toward Long Island. We were traveling at a good speed when we joined a traffic jam on the freeway. We were creeping down the road slower than we could have walked. The tour members were happily talking. They did not feel any pressure that we might miss the plane back to Kiev. There was nothing I could do except to trust the results to God.

Then the traffic cleared and again we were up to speed. We were expected to check in at Aeroflot three hours before the flight.

It was now two hours and fifteen minutes before the flight. At that moment we heard someone wildly honking behind us. It was Roger and the three men in the van. A great sense of relief flooded over me. And then I saw a sign, exit to John F. Kennedy airport. We were almost there.

When we arrived beside the entrance door of the terminal, Roger jumped out first with a group of men designated to unload the luggage from under the bus. On the sidewalk was a horizontal stack of luggage carts locked up until money or a credit card was inserted into the slot. Roger took his credit card and slipped it in again and again, freeing dozens of carts for our people. Sensing the urgency of the situation, they quickly wheeled their belongings through the automatic doors and toward the counter of Aeroflot airlines. Soon there was a line of one hundred people through the hallway ready to be checked. It appeared we were going to make it.

When the process was completed, we bid goodbye to the few people remaining. Sasha Sikorsky would be leaving for Japan as soon as he reached Kiev. God had used him in a marvelous way to establish our church. Now we would need to manage it alone until we found a new Ukrainian pastor. The tour had been our last adventure together.

Roger and I returned to the street. The buses were gone, and the van was parked by the curb. Our last chore was to drive into New York City at rush hour and return the rented harp. What may have seemed to be a frustrating task was like a holiday to us. The Ukrainians were off, safely aboard the aircraft. We drove in silence, without the background noise of Russian and Ukrainian conversation. An impossible dream had come true, and the repercussions from this experience would forever change our lives, the lives of the Ukrainians, and the lives of their new American friends.

Chapter 30

Facing Death

There was one friend who did not go with us on the American tour. Stanislav Pavlenko, our bass soloist, had died three months earlier. I shall never forget that day. Roger was in America, finishing plans for the tour. It was Easter Sunday there. In Kiev the church was worshiping together. Larisa Reutova accompanied the service, and her eldest daughter Sophia played a splendid composition she had written for the postlude. When they returned to the house, their world crashed into despair. Stanislav lay motionless on the floor, his body still warm. When the emergency team arrived, they declared that Stanislav was dead and nothing could be done.

Larisa called me about an hour later. She was crying and talking at the same time, telling me the story in her broken English. "My Stanislav is gone!" she cried hysterically. I was so shocked that I wondered if she really knew what she was saying. I called Sergei Basarab, who talked to her by phone and confirmed the story. Stanislav was dead.

Stanislav had been such a part of our lives. He was so big and strong. He seemed so healthy. Yet a stroke had taken his life at forty-eight years old. I wrote my friends an e-mail and asked for prayers for Larisa and the girls. That night I slept very little. When I finally dozed off, I dreamed that I was in America, going from door to door, weeping as I told my friends about the death of Stanislav.

The next day Sergei Basarab and I went to Larisa's home. I took a dish of macaroni and cheese for the family. When Larisa opened the door, her face was so red from weeping that it matched her hair. She was so glad to see us. I just held her and told her how sorry I was for her loss. I asked her what we could do to help. She said that they were collecting money for funeral expenses: the casket and the burial services. Sergei and I gave from what we had at the moment, and later I sent a donation from the ministry.

Larisa called the girls to come from another apartment because she wanted me to pray with the family. I met Stanislav's sister and his niece and also the aunt who had raised Stanislav as a young boy. The girls, Sophia and Nastia, arrived. Sophia (now age fifteen) was quite distraught. On the day of her father's death, Sophia had been the strong one, according to Larisa. "We must be strong for Daddy," she told those who were grieving. "We must take care of things." Today Sophia's eyes were dark and distant. We just hugged the girls, and their limp bodies leaned against us as if they could be hugged forever.

Larisa said, "I keep expecting to see Stanislav coming through the door." I reassured them that they were not alone, that many people loved them and that God loved them. He would not forsake them. And then we prayed, asking for God's peace, comfort, and blessing upon the family, praising God for the life of Stanislav, and praising Him for the promises of His Word—naming them, claiming them. Larisa seemed peaceful after the prayer. She invited us to the kitchen for coffee, and the girls ate some of the macaroni and cheese.

Larisa started asking me questions: Was it significant that Stanislav had died on a day that is a Resurrection Day in America? Did I believe that the spirit lingers nine days in the house before it departs (a cultural teaching)? I told her that I believed what the Scriptures said, that "to be absent from the body is to be present with the Lord."

"Yes," she said, "when I saw Stanislav's body with his face blue, I knew that wasn't Stanislav any longer. His life is in his spirit, and I haven't felt that his spirit is still here."

As I left, I told Larisa that if she needed me for anything—to pray for her or just hold her hand—just call me. "We don't have to speak the same language," I said. She nodded with tears in her eyes and gave me a hug. Having been Larisa's Bible teacher in Sunday school, I now felt like her pastor as well. I wondered who else, if anyone, was giving her assurance from the Scriptures. I was so inexperienced at such things, yet she had called me, and she knew that I would come to her.

As Sergei and I were walking out of the building, Sergei said, "Did you know that, by Ukrainian custom, Larisa must purchase, cook, and serve all the food for the funeral?"

"No!" I said. "Do you mean like the Ukrainian custom that says one has to cook and serve and entertain at one's own birthday party?" I had never understood why the honored guest has to do all the work.

"Yes," he said, "and this is going to be a big funeral. I don't think Larisa is strong enough to do all the work involved."

"Well, I know who to ask for help," I said. So we called Valentina Yenichek and Eugenia Maksimova, two choir members who were faithful in the church. They agreed to prepare sandwiches and other dishes for two hundred people the following day.

Because Stanislav was a solo artist of the children's opera, the government is supposed to cover most of the funeral expenses. The government was broke, however, and the employees of the theater had not been paid for three months. They had agreed to provide a brass ensemble to play the funeral dirge and two buses to transport the family and guests to the graveside after the funeral. The rest of the expenses Larisa would have to pay. Larisa had no money, but her friends, the choir, and the church raised all the necessary funds. The choir took an offering at rehearsal, and many gave a day's wage to Larisa in a collective offering of $184. When Larisa paid the last funeral bill, she had $1.10 left. She gave glory to God!

I asked Nancy Tyner to accompany me to the funeral. I had never attended a Ukrainian funeral before, though I had witnessed one outside our building in Bereznikee the first winter in Ukraine. It was held on the sidewalk at the main entrance to the building. As I looked out my fifth-floor kitchen window that day, I could see a corpse uncovered in the open coffin. Neighbors had gathered in the snow as a priest stood by the head of the corpse and repeated the liturgy. A collection of brass instrument played the funeral dirge as the coffin was loaded onto a bus. The people followed the bus, leaving flowers strewn along the street. Funerals were often held right there at the apartment buildings. When you saw flowers in the street, you knew that the corpse had been carried there.

Funerals are a joyless affair in Ukraine—no celebration of the life of the deceased, no rejoicing that the dead are with the Lord. Funerals are often held at the place where the departed worked. For Stanislav, this was Children's Opera Theater.

On the following Wednesday, Nancy and I met near the theater and arrived about ten minutes before the funeral. As we entered the foyer of the theater, we saw a black platform in the center of the room where the casket would be placed. There were a few women choir members there—Mila Tretyak and Irina Loktionova. They greeted us and pointed toward the room where the family was. We went in to greet them.

Larisa saw me and immediately came toward me with her arms outstretched saying, "Dianichka," which means "my dear friend Diane." We hugged, and the girls came forward and fell into our arms.

When we returned to the hall, a group of men were carrying Stanislav's corpse, uncovered in a black box. They placed the box on the platform. People began to arrive, placing flowers on the body, which was covered to the chest with a white lace cloth. The family came and took their places by the casket. There was a lot of wailing, but it was not from the family. It was from the first people who had placed flowers in the casket.

Then the recorded music began . . . solemn a cappella music over the sound system. Sometimes there would be a power surge, and the pitch would dip and come back. More and more people arrived, and the hall was packed with over two hundred people standing in a small space. I recognized Lydia Bychkova, Sasha Sikorsky, and our driver, Andre, in the crowd.

We stood for the entire service, which lasted over an hour. The priest, sang the liturgy. I couldn't see very much of the activity of the service because we were all standing on the same level. During the liturgy, however, the priest walked around the casket swinging something. Candles were lit, a red book was kissed by each member of the family, and a seal was placed on Stanislav's forehead. Then the liturgy was finished.

The choir had requested to sing at the funeral. They wanted to show their love to Larisa and Stanislav. Helen Sedih (Music Helen) lifted her hands high into the air above the crowd and the choir sang, from wherever they were in the crowd, two selections from the Rachmaninoff *Solemn Vespers*.

I leaned over to Sasha Sikorsky and asked, "What happens now?"

"We are invited to bid goodbye to Stanislav and to go with him on his way." I was confused. Did that mean that we go up to view the casket? Very few people did. Instead the people near the front started carrying the flower arrangements out of the hall, and the crowd made a path to the door while the recorded music played on. The family said goodbye to Stanislav and came through the pathway toward us until they reached the door. Stanislav's casket was lifted into the air and was carried out of the hall on the shoulders of several men as a brass choir played the funeral dirge. I reached over and hugged Nastia one more time. Larisa was faint and had to breathe smelling salts.

The crowd accompanied the family, following Stanislav "on his way." I decided not to go to the cemetery. I had said all I could say to the family. The burial would be quite a distance from Kiev. So I made my excuses and walked home with Nancy.

Nancy made some tea, and we sat in her kitchen reminiscing about the times with Stanislav. I could see him back in 1992, helping us with the luggage as we departed Kiev and chasing the train to the end of the platform, waving goodbye. I remembered him on the trip to Switzerland as he discovered the West. Nancy talked about his helpfulness the day I went to the hospital and how he had chased her down on the street to tell her how to meet me. Nancy was afraid of this big stranger until he said her name "Nancy," and then she realized who he was. "I like to remember Stanislav the way he was . . . laughing, helpful, sometimes irksome, but we have so many good memories. His last performance in the Faure *Requiem* only a few weeks ago was the best that I had ever heard."

In just a few weeks the Kiev Symphony Orchestra and Chorus would give their first performance in the Kiev Opera Theater—Handel's *Messiah*. Stanislav was to sing the bass solos. Even though other great soloists would perform those solos, I think I will always hear traces of Stanislav's voice in the "Hallelujah Chorus" as he always joined the choir and his cavernous voice amplified the words, "King and Kings, and Lord of Lords. Hallelujah!"

Eight months later, there was another death. Sasha Donskoy's mother had fallen and needed hip-replacement surgery. Because she was a diabetic, they waited until they were sure that her condition was stable, but she died unexpectedly on the operating table.

The family was devastated at the news. They were preparing themselves for the long recuperation Lidia would have as part of her recovery. Lidia had lived with Sasha and Lena from the first day of their marriage. When their children were born, she was the nanny who cooked the meals and took care of the children while the parents worked. Lidia had been an excellent cook, and the family had depended on her for almost everything. Now she was gone.

We called Sasha and Lena to ask if we could come to visit. Lena, through her tears, said, "No, it is better if you don't come. There is so much sadness here."

But Roger could not be denied. He said, "We are coming anyway."

Roger and I arrive at the Donskoy apartment, and we were greeted by the red-eyed family. We hugged them and sympathized with their loss. None of us mentioned the fact that Lidia had professed atheism. Sasha had been faithful to witness to his mother, and she had rejected Sasha's words, but we do not know what had been in her heart. We sat in the living room and looked at pictures of their family. Lidia was in most of them. We encouraged them to talk about their good memories of their mother and grandmother.

As they began to talk, they began to relax, thankful to have friends there with them.

The family insisted that Roger and I stay for dinner. "My mother canned these pickles," Sasha said as he passed the plate to us. "She did all the cooking. Now we must learn to cook for ourselves."

Sasha asked if Roger would preach his mother's funeral. Roger, though ordained a year ago, had never preached a funeral. How would he preach a funeral of someone who had not professed to be a Christian?

Yet he agreed for the sake of Sasha and the family.

Three days later the funeral was held outside the orphanage where Lidia used to work. We were standing in the parking lot amid traces of snow, though most of the landscape was gray. Some of the choir members were there. Many children who remembered Lidia from the orphanage were also there.

We had brought six pink roses. The number of flowers one brings to an event is significant. Odd numbers are for joyful celebrations like birthdays, congratulations, etc. Even numbers are for solemn events such as funerals. Some older ladies who had been Lidia's friends put their flowers in the open casket and wept. Some talked about Lidia with great admiration for her kindness to others, and then the tears and wailing began as they realized she was gone forever.

Finally it was Roger's turn to speak. Roger talked about the love of God and the fact that we are all sinners. He talked to the living who needed a Savior. He told them that Jesus died so that we might live with Him forever, here in this life and for all eternity. The loud weeping stopped, and people listened to his words through Irina Loktionova, his translator. I wondered if the many children, who were standing there in their winter coats and hats, had ever heard about Jesus before. Valentina had told me that when she was growing up in the orphanage, no one was allowed to go to church.

After Roger finished, the family gathered by the casket, and the men carried Lidia in her casket to the funeral bus. The children returned to the orphanage, and the family and friends boarded the bus with the flowers and casket. The bus and cars then departed for the crematorium. Sasha and Lena invited us to ride with them in Sasha's car. We talked very little as we traveled.

We arrived at a compound and followed a gravel road. Several funeral buses were departing from the compound filled with mourners who had left their loved ones at the crematorium. We came to the end of the road where two other groups were lined up for the use of the crematorium. It looked like a large cave of poured cement. From the interior of the cave came recorded music of Albinoni's "Adagio."

Sasha went to get information and came back to say that there would be a forty-five minute wait. Lena was tearful and agitated. "This is our great society," she said sarcastically. "We line up to be born, we line up to be married, and we line up to be buried," she said, wiping her eyes.

Finally it was our turn to enter. The mournful music played from the public address system. I had always loved the melody that was so melancholy but so beautiful. It always made me think of Ukraine and its people. Now here at the crematorium on this gray November day, the music was a picture of sinking, sinking, sinking into death while yearning for life. How final is death.

We stood in the cold, cavernous room. There were no chairs. A small cross adorned the wall in front above the platform that held the casket. The eulogy prepared by the family, was read by the crematorium director. Roger said a few closing words—reading Psalm 23 and a portion of John 14. Then the crematorium director told the people to leave. The music was played again, and the casket was lowered underneath the floor of the platform, in readiness for the next body.

We passed the next group of mourners with their casket as we left the facility and drove to the Donskoy apartment. Preparations had been made to feed all the guests who had traveled to the crematorium. In the living room a long table had been set. Twenty people crowded around it. When they were finished, a second shift of mourners came to share the table. The widowed husband sat in the center with reddened eyes. How would he ever live without his wife of fifty-three years? His friends tried to console him, but he was in shock.

Just our presence was a comfort to Sasha, Lena, Andrew, and Dasha. There were difficult days ahead, but they knew we loved them and would encourage them. In later weeks Sasha's brother, his wife and children, and Sasha's father came to our worship service. Sasha's nephew Zhenya was a fellow student with Dasha in the Accelerated Christian Education program. He was reading the Scriptures every day and was learning about Jesus. A year before his grandmother's death, he had asked to be baptized. He told Sasha Sikorsky he believed in Jesus as his Savior. Could the same thing happen to Sasha's brother's family that happened to Sasha's family? So far it is an unwritten chapter, but God is able.

I wondered about Stanislav—had he ever become a believer? He came to church and at times seemed very warm to the message. Some things we will never know. Sophia, his older daughter, however, wrote me a testimony a few years later that talked about her father. She reminisced about our times in 1992. We were the first Americans her family had ever met. The family knew from the beginning that Roger put God at the center of the music, and this is the reason why his concerts had such unusual joy, expression, and love—because it honored the Creator. She wrote:

> My parents were among the first Ukrainians who met Roger. From the beginning they felt united with him through great spiritual music in spite of a barrier of language. The period of association with Roger was the last and probably the brightest period in the life of my father, when he reached his best performance in the Faure *Requiem* and when he came to God. Roger, a real example of Christian love to all people, persuaded my father in the truth of real faith in Christ. In the last years my father often opened the Bible, reading it not only at home but also during breaks in the times of studying new music for Roger's concerts.

Diane was with us in the most tragic moment in the life of our family—when our father passed away. Together Roger and Diane helped us in the days that followed to get new strength for a new life, supporting our faith, and personally offering their comfort and financial help. We wish the blessings of God to these wonderful people.

We could not separate Larisa and the girls only four months after Stanislav's death. Therefore we took the girls with Larisa on the American tour of 1996. Nastia sold programs in her cute Ukrainian costume, and Sophia impressed the audience as she performed her own compositions on the piano.

A year later Sophia was becoming a leader of our church youth group, always present at the Bible studies. She composed many pieces after her father's death that showed great depth of feeling and maturity of soul. She even began working on a youth musical based upon the Christmas story in the Gospel of Luke.

Another Christmas passed, and Roger and I again traveled to the United States for our annual board meeting and fundraising activities. Support for the mission had grown tremendously since the tour. We were excited about the eighty widows who were receiving food. We named the program "The Myrtle McMurrin Food Project" after Roger's mother. We told Mom McMurrin about it as we visited her in Ohio. We had little time to visit, only one day, and then we rushed to Florida for the meeting. We would be coming back to her house at the end of our six weeks of travel.

Two weeks later we received the news that Roger's mother was in the hospital. She had suffered a serious heart attack. Roger immediately flew to Ohio to be by her bedside with the rest of his brothers and his sister. Three days later she quietly passed on to her eternal reward. Mom had lived ninety years, she loved the Lord, and her homegoing was a celebration.

When we returned to Kiev, our Ukrainian friends were very concerned about Roger's losing his mother. They marveled at the peace and assurance he showed when others talked about her. He told them his mother was in heaven, and he was so thankful that he had been in the States to spend her last hours with her.

Roger and I saw an opportunity to model for our Ukrainian friends how a Christian faces the death of a loved one. We organized a memorial service for Myrtle McMurrin and invited the choir and orchestra to participate. We also invited the church congregation and all the widows who were being served by them. This lady, who had helped us begin our ministry to Ukraine with her funds and prayers and her name, would be a testimony to all of a Christian life and death.

Roger's brother Lee, sister Norma, and brother-in-law Don came to Kiev to participate in the service. Over three hundred people came, including more than twenty widows whom we had never met. Roger preached a sermon entitled, "How a Christian Faces Death." It was a solemn service but demonstrated a holy joy of knowing God's promises for eternal life are true for the believer. The choir and orchestra performed pieces from the Brahms *Requiem:* "How Lovely Is Thy Dwelling Place" and another movement that focused on "Joy Everlasting."

The focus was God's grace. Though moments from Mother's life were shared, she was not glorified, only Christ was. The tales of her experiences of faith had a significant effect on many lives that day. Many of the widows who were present began coming to church after that day, and several of them came to faith in Christ. They wanted to know that joy and hope that was evident in the lives of her family. The service had even ended with the "Hallelujah Chorus" and "When the Saints Go Marchin' In," further proclaiming that one need not fear death.

As Mom McMurrin said of her death in a last letter, "Don't grieve for me. I'm only changing addresses."

Chapter 31

The Language of Music

When God called Roger and me to Kiev, he called musicians. Why has music been so important in changing lives? How does that happen?

To many Americans, classical music is an experience of black and white with various shades of gray. But to Ukrainians, this same music from the masters of the seventeenth to twentieth centuries is gold and red, Persian blue, lime green, delicate pink, and deep plum. It is as if Ukrainians have musical antennae to receive the nuance of emotion that others cannot.

Even before communist times, Ukrainian heroes were writers, poets, and musicians. That is why artistic expression was highly restricted by the Communists. Music about religious subjects was forbidden for seventy years. Why? Because music affects the Ukrainian soul.

In the apartment of a typical Ukrainian family, the most treasured possessions are a collection of books and, perhaps, old phonograph recordings. In a country where the love of the arts and music is deeply rooted in the people, the stage was set for a spiritual awakening through the new musical pieces we brought to them—masterpieces that tell about God's judgment for sin and His mercy to all who believe. The attributes of God are described in the language of music: power, peace, compassion, justice, majesty, and blessing. Music is a vehicle to see God, though all who listen do not "see" Him with their ears. It is a mystery that is difficult to explain.

In an American concert hall, many people come for entertainment. In Ukraine, the people come for edification. What is the difference? Ukrainians yearn for something beyond the dreariness of their mundane lives. They want to glean something mystical that relates to their souls. Most Ukrainians are interested in this, even atheists. The word "soul" and "spiritual" is used by both to explain what is missing in their lives. They come expecting an experience that will make them more noble, more educated, and more cultured. They seek it through live musical performances, theater, and museums.

In America, entertainment is linked to pop culture. Even in most worship services, pop culture has become the normal musical expression. It often focuses on the human experience through a simplistic sentimentality. Ukrainians prefer a more complex, creative beauty reflecting the Creator of the universe. The awe of Isaiah who saw the Lord "high and lifted up" . . . this is what the Ukrainian soul is searching for.

Enter Roger and Diane . . . two Christians who share this music and its message.

First of all, just because we are Americans, we are a novelty. Why did these Americans leave America, the land of opportunity? Why Ukraine? It is the question most asked by newspaper reporters, television anchormen, and people on the street.

Second, the music is unlike anything they have heard before—choir and orchestra together performing religious music from honored composers. Choir members are touched by singing it. God's power is in this music. He becomes real to them through the divine spark of creativity that ordained it. Each time they sing this music, they rediscover that creativity, led by a conductor who believes its message.

In the movie *Chariots of Fire,* Eric Liddel, a Christian who won a gold medal in the 1924 Olympic games for the 400 meters, said of his gift of running: "When I run, I feel His pleasure." And so it is with musician and conductor. In the performance of the music, they receive the gift of feeling God's splendor. It is an experience with God Himself through the music. As Sasha Donskoy has said,

"Our concerts are more like worship services than ordinary musical performances."

This music is fascinating to Ukrainian concertgoers too. All of their Ukrainian traditional church music is a cappella. This new sound, performed by a huge chorus of 115 singers (the largest chorus in Ukraine) and orchestra is overwhelming. "I cannot live without your music," says Luda, a Ukrainian woman who has come to Christ. "I bring all my friends so they can experience God the way I experience Him in your concerts."

Even though the concerts may be sung in English or German or Latin, the experience is beyond words: The nuances of expression, the emotion of the phrases, the dramatic contrasts that cause shivers across the back of the neck and the heart to pound. Ukrainians experience the rainbow of musical expression, and it is felt not just by the ears but also by the mind, emotion, and even the physical body.

The concerts are a great experience, but that experience eventually wanes. Eric Liddell said to a group of fans, "Today you came to see a race. You thrilled to see the winner approach the finish line, and you shared in his elation. But then you go home, and life goes on as usual. I wish something more for you—something lasting!"

For Music Mission Kiev, this musical experience leads to the mission of our church: Church of the Holy Trinity. It began with a group of musicians who accepted Jesus Christ and were transformed by His Holy Spirit. It attracts those who have come to the concerts and want to know more about this God who is able to save sinners and give mercy to those who believe. On the Sunday after a concert performance, the visitor ratio soars. Some come out of curiosity, some come out of spiritual need. All are welcomed.

Church of the Holy Trinity is a permanent place to connect with the Almighty in worship, praise, preaching, the study of God's Word, and fellowship with believers through the Holy Spirit. It provides a refuge for the lost, food for the hungry, hope for the oppressed. Rather than the musical concert becoming the extension of a church—our church is the extension of the concert experience. Music Mission Kiev, as the organization is called, is exactly this: Music leads Mission in Kiev. The focus is music. The result is changed lives, discipleship, and service.

Chapter 32

Thorns in the Flesh

In the years that we have been in Ukraine, we have known the experience of spiritual warfare as we become more committed to God's calling. The conflicts that we have encountered are three basic types: health, daily living, and political barriers.

The struggles of daily living were most intense in the first two years when we were renting the apartment across the river. Finding food and supplies, furnishing a home, and traveling with difficulty were the most obvious then. Loneliness for American friends and dreariness of our surroundings were emotional trials. Many of these problems were solved by moving to the center of the city. We still had frustrations, but life was easier.

The political problems were always with us, and we had to keep a sense of humor not to become discouraged. We are the only private, self-supporting musical enterprise in Ukraine and are therefore in competition with the government. Some of our pressures included the unexpected increases of concert hall rent, harassment in renewing visas and foreign-resident registrations, and the jealousy of some other Ukrainian conductors who would punish our singers for their participation in our activities. The popularity of our concerts, the news media's interest in our music and Christian witness, and our outreach to the poor of Ukraine, has brought us enough positive publicity that the Ukrainian government allows us to exist. We have no legal status as a music organization, and the government could close us down at any time, but in God's grace, that has not happened.

The health problems grew more troublesome with time. At first there were the flus and colds of adjusting to a new climate. Since we had lived in Florida for almost twenty years, the winter was a shock to our bodies. Two debilitating conditions for Roger, however, started in January 1994—migraine headaches and shoulder pain.

The morning after a successful concert, Roger would often be kept motionless by a migraine headache that could last from five to fourteen hours. During this time he was unable to do anything— business work, rehearsal, Bible study teaching. During our years in Ukraine, the headaches became more frequent. At first he suffered about one every month. By 1997, however, Roger battled two every week.

As for me, Sunday mornings were difficult. As I would prepare for my Bible class, I was often overcome by a cloud of depression, sometimes nausea, accompanied by physical weakness. I forced myself to go to church, even though I was sometimes so dizzy that I could hardly walk. I climbed the four flights of stairs and greeted my class in the large room. As I began to teach, the feeling would ease. By the end of the lesson, it was gone. It was not stagefright or guilt for not being prepared. I have never been nervous talking in front of a crowd, and my lessons were always complete. It was a discouragement brought on by a spiritual source. It made me more determined than ever to fight the battle and get to church.

Another trial for Roger was the pain in his shoulders. We tried many doctors and health experts in Ukraine. Many recommended massage, which helped, but the pain was so deep in the joints that nothing could entirely relieve the condition. We had Roger's neck X-rayed. The doctor there said his neck was in deplorable condition, and that was causing his shoulder pain. We started seeing a chiropractor when we were in the States, but the old problem still continued.

Some of the remedies were strange. One day I came home to see Roger lying on the dining room table and a man heating glass vials and placing them on Roger's back. Another man rubbed his back with kerosene. Others recommended vodka poultices or urine poultices, or even drinking your own urine. If that didn't work, he should go to the village and counsel with the oldest *babushka* (grandmother).

Eventually Roger couldn't sleep at night because the pain would wake him up. The only solution was to take injections by our friend Dr. Zhivago once every three months. The doctor warned him that he could not take the injections forever.

One of our friends said to us at dinner one night, "How cruel God must be to give you pain in your shoulders, the very place that a conductor needs movement and freedom." Yet we knew that, although God was allowing this pain, He was not the author of it. Satan was trying to inhibit what we did in the musical realm, and there would be eventual victory.

In June 1997, Roger was rehearsing the *1812 Overture* by Tchaikovsky with the orchestra. It was another premiere work because the Communists disallowed the recurring theme "God Save the Tzar" and rewrote the music to satisfy their doctrines. As Roger made a dramatic cut-off, a bicep muscle in his right arm broke from its connective bone and it fell into a lump around his elbow.

Not only was his muscular activity degenerating but so was his physical energy. Roger was delegating more activity to his Ukrainian associates. After working all day in the office, he would become so tired that he was unable to conduct the evening rehearsal. A man who usually enjoyed an incredibly high energy level, Roger was sinking into periods where he was not able to accomplish what he used to do. He had three or four able choir members who could conduct for him. His mind could be at rest that they would accomplish the goals for the rehearsal.

He was still preaching and teaching in the church, but he no longer cooked the church meal afterwards. This fellowship dinner had been meeting at our home ever since we had moved to the city. At first Roger and I cooked for forty, fifty, or sixty people every week. Then he found Sasha Bichkov. Sasha was a tenor in the choir, a dedicated Christian, and a former army cook. Roger taught him the recipes he wanted, and Sasha enjoyed serving in this way. By the end of the year Sasha was cooking for eighty-two people. Sasha, who had been brought to faith by his grandmother, had been looking for a church where he could study the Bible. He found that in the Church of the Holy Trinity and served there with great joy.

One of the reasons why the number at the church dinner expanded from forty to eighty-two people in one year was the outreach ministries that were developing. The newest group in our church was a youth ministry for students aged thirteen to twenty. Two young seminary students (Yegor and Max) came to lead the teenagers who were finding the answers to life in the Scriptures and enjoying wholesome fun and friendship with each other. They met for frequent gatherings at the McMurrins' apartment.

Another growing outreach was the widows' program. From twenty widows in December 1995 to eighty widows in December 1996, the number continued to rise to 115 widows by December 1997. This required many volunteers, as well as paid supervisors. Assisting Valentina Yenichek was Allah Mokrenko.

Allah had retired from the Opera Chorus when she came to sing for us in 1993. She is a tireless worker who is always joyful. Like many others, she found a relationship with Christ when she came to our choir. In her own words, she says:

> I took Christ into my heart when I was over fifty years old. Before that there were many years of unknown. I did not know anything about God, anything about the Bible, anything about religion in general. Moreover, talking about religion in our Communist society was banned. I was raised up in this way.
>
> Once I heard from my fellows from the choir that an American, Roger McMurrin, would be moving to Kiev, and he would be forming a choir to perform classical, Western "spiritual" music, never heard before in Ukraine. By the way, the word "spiritual" was also banned. Though we knew there was this music, it was impossible to receive it in our country.
>
> Roger listened to my audition and accepted me into his choir. The music he presented filled my mind with thoughts about God. The beautiful music was full of praise to the Lord. The words were taken from the Bible. I felt like I needed to study the Bible. But where? How?
>
> When Diane McMurrin started a Bible study group, I went there each week and stayed afterward for the weekly worship

services of Church of the Holy Trinity where Roger preached. All of these experiences brought me to a realization that God had touched my life—I know the Lord. I believed that Jesus saved me, and I needed to be baptized. So I did. Now and always I will praise the Lord forever and ever.

I remember the day Allah was baptized. It was our first baptism by sprinkling and Roger's first baptism to administer. With tear-filled eyes, Allah raised her head at the conclusion of the sacrament and asked Roger, "May I say something now?"

With Roger's permission she turned and faced the congregation. She spoke to them about her love for Christ and how she wished that everyone could trust in Jesus and be saved. It was a moment so sincere, so unique, that I will never forget the warmth of the Spirit of God in that room as Allah, a lady in her fifties, spoke of being "born again."

From 1995 to 1997, the number of employees for our ministry grew from four to twenty-four. They were not paid large salaries, but they performed important functions every week. Allah, for instance, worked for two full days a week with the widows and church suppers and was paid twenty-five dollars a month.

Roger and I returned to the United States in August 1997 for fundraising and visiting family. I went to visit my mother who had now become a patient in an Alzheimer's unit. The past six months showed a drastic decline in her condition. Six months ago she had been in an apartment with her husband. Now she lived in a unit where she was fading from reality and being fed by an attendant. I spent much of the day just sitting with her, holding her hand. "When are you coming back?" she had asked me as I left that day in 1993. That day was gone. Even if I returned to America, our relationship would never be the same. I realized that the next time I saw her, she would probably not know who I was. And from Alzheimer's disease, there is no "coming back."

In Ukraine, I thought of Mother many times. I grieved that our relationship would never be the same. She was dying slowly, and there was nothing I could do to stop it. I couldn't even be with her. Yet I knew she was receiving the best of care. I called her a few times, and she was able to talk, but all she could say was "Yes." Afterwards, they said she didn't know that I had called but sometimes she would talk to my photograph pinned to her bulletin board in her room.

In the beginning days of our ministry, she had sent us her social security check every month. She had read every word of our missionary encounters and even underlined passages to pray about. She wrote me faxes every week. But now she could no longer read or write. How I longed to share with her what God was doing in our lives. That will have to wait until we meet each other in heaven.

Our last stop on our American trip was California. Through friends, Max and Lois Rondoni, we were introduced to a surgeon who specialized in shoulder surgery. Dr. Scott Southard, a forty-year-old surgeon, had performed over six thousand operations. He had served on the medical mission field both in Vietnam and Africa. Knowing we were missionaries and wanting to help, he examined Roger and told him that his condition could wait no longer.

The MRI test he ordered for the next day revealed that both shoulders were in trouble, but the right one was extremely damaged. Both shoulders had bone spurs piercing the muscles beneath like two giant thorns. No wonder Roger had been in such pain! These thorns must be removed and the muscles repaired. Scott strongly urged that we have the surgery when we returned in January, arthoscopic on the left shoulder and general surgery on the right. We agreed.

Returning to Kiev, we felt that we had hope for Roger's condition. The MRI had shown exactly what was going on inside Roger's body. There was no doubt about the need for surgery. It would be a tedious recovery, but God had again provided the victory. Roger could be restored and continue the musical conducting he loved so much.

Presenting a concert in Ukraine had enough difficulties without impinged shoulders. We were facing five concerts before January, three of them Christmas concerts. Every concert has its warfare, but one concert will always live in my memory. It was January 1997. Andre was still working for us as a part-time administrator, and we had a little Ford automobile. For the first time, our Christmas concert was being taped and produced for national television at the Dome Organi Musiki.

This concert had been scheduled for December in preparation for American Christmas Day on December 25. Then the officials had changed the date to January and given us a Saturday night, which meant that many of our regular orchestra players would not be able to perform with us. We usually have concerts on Monday, the night the Opera House is closed, so that we can get the best string players in the city. This January date was not too late for Ukrainian Christmas, however. In fact it was scheduled to be broadcast on Ukrainian Christmas Eve.

It had been a hectic day. We had many loose ends for the evening performance, such as orchestra personnel problems and missing music. Andre had forgotten to get the money at the bank for the orchestra, and we had to persuade the bank to open after hours to give us our money. Then the leaders at the Dome Organi Musiki told us we would not be able to have the hall until 5:00 P.M.

We had already scheduled television interviews and a choir and orchestra rehearsal to begin there at 2:00 P.M. The orchestra players who were performing with us for the first time needed another full rehearsal. Now that opportunity was gone. Two hours was very little time to get ready for the concert.

All day the temperature had been so cold. We had been living in the smallest room in the apartment with our two electric heaters. Roger had bronchitis, a terrible cough, weakness, and watery eyes.

The sidewalk and hall of our building was covered with gray, dirty snow that was continually tracked into our apartment. People were coming and going all day with problems to be solved. I just wanted to bury my head and wait for tomorrow.

At 4:00 P.M., however, I agreed to go with Roger to the Dome Organi Musiki. Andre had forgotten to wear his suit and tie as Roger had requested, so he drove home in our car to get dressed. Roger and I had to get a taxi and carry seven hundred programs, seven hundred brochures, a conducting stand, the orchestra music, the pewpeeters (thirty wire, folding music stands in one huge potato sack), Roger's clothes for the concert, 120 candles for the choir, and my thermos of coffee. At first the taxi driver had quoted a $3 fee for the ride, but after we had loaded all this stuff, he charged us $5.

I said angrily to Roger, "Why do *we* have to do all this when you have a staff and 115 choir members who could help us? We're even carrying choir folders for choir members who were too lazy to pick them up at the rehearsal hall!" I get overburdened for Roger and end up being more of a burden for him with my criticisms.

"You know that it's always this way, always has been," said Roger. "The director has to do everything."

"But it *can* change," I said, and then I bit my tongue rather than continue the battle.

When we arrived at the hall, the TV truck was parked right out front. This was going to be a professional operation. We unloaded the taxi at the rear entrance in the snow, leaving everything stacked inside the door. A few choir members who had arrived early helped us carry the materials to the appropriate places.

At 5:00 P.M. we were allowed to enter the hall, and it was total chaos. Television crews were setting up seven cameras and all the paraphernalia that went with them. There were twenty people stringing cables everywhere. The choir and orchestra were doing a "start and stop" rehearsal with Roger. The children's choir was running through the hall with their chaperones. When the organist got lost in the music and the brass instruments played the wrong notes, I could no longer handle the stress. I got up from my seat and walked outside.

I found a little German supermarket and bought some salami and potato chips. I behaved like a glutton, devouring them furiously on my way back to the hall. I nervously wondered how this night would end.

As the crowd began to arrive, I waited at the front entrance. Some Americans had reserved tickets to be picked up from me at the door. There is no service window. Reserved tickets require a person to wait in the cold foyer and hand the customer the tickets as they appear at the door. After forty minutes, the Americans arrived, three minutes before the concert was to begin.

I went to find my seat in the hall. A woman was sitting in it without a ticket. She didn't want to move. A friend of hers, also without a ticket, had poached the seat next to mine. Finally, they got up and moved to two other prime seats.

I heard the a cappella processional number being sung at the rear of the hall. The concert was beginning. Then I noticed the orchestra was not in place. They weren't even in the room. My heart was pounding. How would they be able to enter the crowded chancel once the 115 choir members were in place? The choir, carrying candles, was processing down the center aisle when the first orchestra player appeared. He summoned the others, and fifty-five more players sneaked to their places, crawling over chairs and microphones, as the choir paused in the center aisle singing thirty repetitions of an "Alleluia" phrase. Thinking of the television cameras, I was dying inside. What next? The orchestra didn't even have a chance to tune.

In spite of this ominous beginning, the concert was glorious. The soloists were spectacular; the children's choir tone was pure crystal; the choir was sensitive and rich; and the orchestra did OK.

Roger conducted the numbers with full control of all the forces, although his color was pale gray, and he was running a fever. The perspiration visibly flew from his brow. His deep concentration would not acknowledge his ailments.

The concert ended with the "Hallelujah Chorus" and thunderous applause. The room was quite cold. No one had taken off their coats. The warmth of spirit, however, was reflected in many smiles and cheers. Twenty minutes later the crowd was gone, and the electrician turned out the overhead lights.

Roger sat in the front row, cold and wet, wrapped in his wool overcoat with a neck scarf over his damp hair. The TV crew was setting up for the interview he was to have given before the concert. They focused their lights on a Christmas tree, which would serve as the background for the set.

"I can't do this," Roger said to me, his voice practically gone from laryngitis. "You will have to give this interview. I am just too sick." He looked like a lifeless lump of clay bent over in the straight-backed chair.

"Roger," I said, "you *have* to do this. You conducted the concert. Who else can give the commentary you need on the program? Nothing else makes sense."

He nodded, took off his coat and scarf, and slowly walked into the set to the center chair where Natasha, a lovely Ukrainian lady, was waiting to begin. Sergei Basarab was seated to his other side as his translator.

Natasha spoke personally with him before the interview, saying, "Mr. McMurrin, we could talk about the concert or the lovely music you perform, but what I really want to talk about is God."

Roger got his voice back. He no longer felt tired. What an opportunity!

At that moment, sitting in the cold, dark cathedral, I knew why we had had so many barriers of sickness and frustration. Here was an open door to speak about the Lord on national television to 60 million Ukrainians. Natasha's last question was "Mr. McMurrin, at this Christmastime, do you have a special message for the Ukrainian people?"

Yes, such moments are like being on a mountaintop, even though it feels like we're "rolling a boulder uphill" to get there. There is spiritual warfare, but the Lord Jesus Christ holds the victory in every situation.

This was the first of many broadcasts of our music. There were sponsors in Ukraine that wanted to be identified with our concerts. Yet the struggles of that first concert were more intense than any of the other concerts.

Sitting in the dark cathedral behind the cameras that night, watching Roger talk about God's gift of salvation through Jesus Christ, I felt the presence of the Lord, softly encircling my soul, and a quiet voice deep inside me said, "Tell the story. This is why I brought you here."

Chapter 33
A Christmas Reunion

Christmas 1997 was very special. This was our fifth Christmas in Kiev. Matthew was coming back to spend the holidays with us. Nothing could have pleased us more. Matthew had been so much a part of our work in Kiev from the beginning. His Christmas break from Montreat College, in Black Mountain, North Carolina, provided us three whole weeks together. Now a sophomore, he was studying music and planning to return to Kiev someday either in music or in ministry or both.

It had been difficult for our other son, Marc, to understand how we could leave him and his family for five years. We had arranged for him to come to visit in March. In the short week he was here, he experienced the church, attended one of our concerts, and formed friendships among the Ukrainian people. Thus he gained an understanding and appreciation of our calling and mission work.

Matthew arrived with three large suitcases. Two of them were full of gifts from America: scarves for the widows and slippers for the young orphans whom we had been helping. At the edge of the city there is an orphanage for 160 very young children, ages three months to three years of age. Through the Church of the Holy Trinity, we have an employee who works at the orphanage to bring Jesus' love to the children. She also makes the orphanage accountable that all the aid we send is used for the proper purposes and not sold for personal benefit. When we learned that the children had few slippers, many in sizes too large for them, we wanted to help. No longer would they be wearing large slippers tied to their tiny feet.

Matthew went with us to the orphanage, and the three of us sat on the floor playing with the little two year olds. Some of them suffered from Down's syndrome or syphilis. All were precious.

The orphanage was guarded about our involvement with the children. We were still trying to win their trust. There had been two crib deaths, so we were not allowed to go into the infant room.

Matthew was with us in Kiev for our third Christmas concert that month. The carols that we had introduced four years ago were now familiar to many Ukrainian ears, and they came to experience them again. Realizing that this would be Roger's last concert to conduct until after his shoulder surgery, one widow who attended the concert said, "I hope that I live long enough to see you conduct again."

We had wonderful times with Matthew, reminiscing about our adventures in Ukraine. After five years Kiev seemed so different now. We had a comfortable apartment, a growing church, and a marvelous choir and orchestra (many of whom had toured America with us). God had blessed us so!

Matthew's fluency in Russian had not diminished. He was able to talk to everyone, which made us question why we were so slow at language. After all, we had been here twice as long as Matthew.

With our youth leaders on college vacation, Matthew took over the teaching of the young people. He enjoyed the group that had been drawn to our church, and they shared special times together.

During Advent many people desired membership in Church of the Holy Trinity. We had not talked much about this to our congregation, but when we did give an opportunity, seventy-three people filled out applications and came forward publicly to repeat their vows of faith. Widows, young people, musicians, and people from all walks of life joined the large circle that extended around the entire room. The church had a new surge of significance in the lives of the people.

Lydia Bychkova had still not joined the church or been baptized. One of her dreams has come true, however. Roger established a talent agency called Taras-Mak, independent of the mission organization. Through this agency, Ukrainian talent could find opportunity for performances in the West—singers, conductors, ensembles, and child prodigies. There was a gathering held on Christmas week at our apartment, and many of the talent of this new company were there. Lydia and I talked about past times—the early days, how our lives had changed during the years. She had sold the apartment she had been living in and found a less expensive one where she lived with her ailing mother. I feel that God is still calling her to Himself.

On Christmas Eve and Christmas Day we invited the choir to our apartment for a party. The choir is so big that we could not entertain them all at one time, so the sopranos and tenors came the first night, and the altos and basses came on Christmas Day.

I talked to several people about how they felt about their lives now, five years into our experiences together. What were their meaningful memories and realized dreams?

Some of them spoke spontaneously; others gave thought to the question and returned written responses.

Sergei Baoaroh, the former atheist-agnostic translator who had persistently asked Roger to start the church— and who had become a Christian in that very setting—said, "We now have a *real* Christian community. It is not an empty set of rituals but a living, loving relationship among God's people, serving Him as we serve each other and reaching out with the Gospel."

Larisa Reutova, our Larisa the Red, said, "From the moment I met Roger, we had an understanding based upon our love of music. My joy has been to work with him—experiencing that music. Roger has shown us that we can accomplish anything if we work hard. After all, we prepared those first two concerts in 1992 in only twenty days. God is in our music, and the Lord is near to me, especially since the death of Stanislav."

Helen Sedih (Music Helen), whom we met at George McCammon's church in 1993, is now helping us publish our new hymnal for our church. It is a comprehensive book of the great hymns of Europe and America translated into Ukrainian and traditional favorites of the Ukrainian culture. She wrote:

> Although I was raised in an Orthodox family and my grandfather was a priest, I did not understand who God is. I did not have that spiritual link between the church, myself, and Christ. When the McMurrins came and I started to work with Roger, I began to know Jesus as my Savior. I looked in the Bible for the answers to my questions. Then God changed my life as He changed my attitudes and goals for the future.
>
> At our last worship service, the whole choir and orchestra came to sing and play the "Hallelujah Chorus" and "O Come All Ye Faithful." At the end of the service, we lit candles with the congregation and together sang "Silent Night." Many choir members told me that this was a special time for them as they remembered how God had entered their lives through their experiences with Roger. I thank the Lord for sending the McMurrin family who, with Christ's help, changes the lives of Ukrainian people like me.

Michael Dorogoi, the bass singer from 1992 who reminded me of a prince, bowing and greeting me with his formal "Good evening," had brought his friends to choir and to church. His Christian faith had visibly bloomed in the past five years. Already he was showing signs of leadership for the future of the church, even leading a Bible study by himself. He wrote:

> Praise the Lord that He gave me the opportunity to meet Roger. Through his preaching I believed in Christ who forgave my sins by dying on the cross. Before, my life was filled with anxiety and problems about my daughters. We argued and were always in conflict. Then when I discovered more about the power of sin, and how God forgives us, I was calm from that moment on. I have received peace in my heart and patience in my circumstances. When I went to America on tour, the Americans' sincere joy and acceptance ministered to my

heart. Now I am happy . . . happy that I will live forever with my Lord Jesus Christ. I continue to read my Bible to understand His plan for me. My hope is in His eternal Word.

Sasha Donskoy was there with Lena, Andrew, and Dasha. How much they had become a part of our lives. Sasha was excited about his new project: Finding land in Kiev to build a Christian center for our church—ten acres that would hold a church sanctuary to seat 1,800 people, where our choir could perform concerts and invite the audience back to the same place for worship services. The complex would include facilities for Sunday school, Christian day school, a Bible college, and a seminary. There would be a gymnasium for recreation for youth and all ages. A fellowship hall for five hundred people would replace our Sunday night dinners at the apartment. Christian groups could hold conferences, and the widows' ministry could be conducted on an even larger scale. Also there would be a Christian hospital where Western doctors could come to train Ukrainian doctors in much needed procedures. A guesthouse would provide accommodations for the doctors and other visiting teachers who were there for leadership. Sasha and Roger went into a corner to look over some proposals and talk about their dream.

An impossible dream? No, another adventure of faith. God had taught us in Ukraine that if our faith is to grow, we must trust Him for something larger than ourselves. He is able to bring it to pass. And we walk forward, believing. Our whole history in Ukraine has been trusting Him in faith. His work is glorious in our eyes.

The last letter I received was from Irina Loktionova, the lovely singer who wrote the first tribute on Roger's birthday back in 1992. Now she was by my side every Sunday, translating the Bible lessons I taught to a large circle of ladies. Her letter is an example of how a Christian grows up in his or her faith. To my amazement, these Ukrainians mature very fast spiritually, probably because their lives are so full of conflict that they have to depend upon the Lord for daily survival. She writes:

Dear Diana,

I cannot say in one letter all the good things you brought to us. As for the very beginning, when you just came and started your work in Kiev, I can tell you that those were the most wonderful days in my life. Even this mental picture is dear to my heart: those Bible study nights when we were sitting in the warm, cozy room in Bereznikee, where you met us with such love and hospitality . . . our calm talks, after which we were full of joy and love. We felt that all of us were one family.

Many of us were baptized in childhood, the only thin thread that connected us with Christianity. We could not say we were strong atheists because thoughts about God's punishment were always in our minds. If we met a wicked man or saw something unfair, we always said, "God will punish those people." Also we know that our deeds were not so good as they ought to be. That's why when I came to your Bible classes for the first time and Roger asked me "Are you sure you'll be in heaven after your death?", I answered with strong confidence, "I'll be in hell." I knew that all my bad deeds are counted by the Almighty Ruler.

But you opened our eyes, showing us that God is not only the Righteous Judge, but He is also loving and forgiving. He is looking for His lost children and wants to lead us in the right way. I liked the fact that everything you did was without any pressure on anybody—with tact, love, and care. Now when I look back on those days, I see all of us, your pupils, with our naive and maybe silly questions, but you explained everything to us with such patience and understanding. You taught us and led us. As for me, the most important influence on my life was seeing you live the Christian life. Others can talk about spiritual things, but you showed us how to live.

Like others, I accepted Jesus into my life after you and Roger came to Kiev, but this change was not easy. I took many wrong steps in my new Christian walk. For example I immediately started sharing my thoughts about Christ with many people. Some of my friends were happy to talk about heaven, salvation, church, etc. because they now had the freedom to express ideas. Some were comforted from their sorrow, and their eyes came alive with hope. I felt great exaltation.

If someone argued with me, however, I felt angry and defeated. Such was the case with my friend Natasha. She and her brother had their own convictions about the way of salvation, true faith, worship service, etc. So I immediately forgot the main commandments—"love your neighbor" and even more "love your enemy"—and started my fearless fight against such wrong thoughts and superstitions.

Now I understand that I was wrong. During that time I could not do anything. I couldn't convince them. I was without a "sword and shield." It was silly to start such a struggle. I also forgot that His Word, patience, and peace can overcome any barrier.

Maybe, due to our painful mistakes, we begin to understand things that you taught us. First to remember that we are "salt of the earth" and that "Christ has not brought peace on earth but a sword." (We must fight evil.) We should not forget the main thing—"overcome evil with good." I am very grateful for all your prayers and your patience because you bring us up like we are children. I also try to be tolerant and not to try to change people in my own strength. I must do what I can. The result will be only in His hands. It does not depend upon me. Only God can change people and fill their hearts with joy and peace.

You presented us with Bibles—it was the lift. Some of us had never even seen this book before and knew nothing about it. To receive such a precious treasure from your hands was really a holiday for our souls. Now we could study this book—His Word—to learn the real truth. It opened our eyes to facts we had never heard. It told us who our Creator is. Step by step, we came to know more about Christ and His love for us sinners and to know that our sin might be forgiven through our faith in Him.

God knows everything, and I hope that we will see the fruit of your holy work here in Kiev. You nurtured not only that small group of people who were seated in your living room. Your influence has touched many hearts. Your presence with us has brought God's music to our souls. Its splendor has changed our lives. And it will change many more, because God is working His purpose in Ukraine.

Sincerely,
Irina

There is a melody playing in the distance, drawing people toward the source of the music. It is God's music. It began the day of creation with the music of the spheres. With a great crescendo it broke forth in beautiful light that first Christmas night with the angel choirs singing, "Glory to God in the highest and on earth, peace, goodwill toward men."

The splendor of His music calls to hearts, singing the glorious message, "For unto *you* is born this day . . . a Savior which is Christ the Lord." And it dawns upon souls one by one, gathering people from every nation, tongue, and tribe, where one day they shall sing in a mighty chorus around God's eternal throne:

Worthy is the Lamb that was slain, and hath redeemed us to God by His blood, to receive power and riches and wisdom and strength and honor and glory and blessing.

Listen! Can you hear it? It is more than words, more than notes. It is the splendor of His music.

Appendix

A list of musical works premiered and presented by the Kiev Symphony Orchestra and Chorus in Ukraine

Albinoni, Thomaso	"Adagio"
Anderson, LeRoy	Blue Tango, Bugler's Holiday, Fiddle Faddle, Jazz Pizzicato, Sleigh Ride
Bach, J. S.	Cantata #4: Christ Lag in Todesponden (Christ Lay in the Bonds of Death)
	Cantata #140 Wachet Auf (Sleepers Wake)
	Come Sweet Death
	"Jesu, Joy of Man's Desiring" from Cantata 147
	Mass in B Minor
	Magnificat
	Passion According to St. Matthew
Barber, Samuel	Adagio for Strings
Beethoven, Ludwig van	Choral Fantasy
	"Hallelujah" from the Mount of Olives
Berlioz, Hector	Requiem
	"Roman Carnival Overture"
Bernstein, Leonard	Chichester Psalms
Bish, Diane	Morning Has Broken (excerpts)
Brahms, Johannes	Ein Deutches Requiem (A German Requiem)
Britten, Benjamin	A Ceremony of Carols
Copland, Aaron	Appalachian Spring
	Rodeo
	"The Lark"

Durufle, Maurice	Requiem
Faure, Gabrielle	Requiem
	"Pavanne"
Gershwin, George	Medley
	Rhapsody in Blue
Handel, George F.	Messiah
Honegger, Artur	Cantique de Noel (Christmas Cantata)
Mozart, W. A.	Requiem*
	"Ave Verum"*
	"Gloria in Excelsis"
Mendelssohn, Felix	Elijah
	Lobgesang (Hymn of Praise)
Menotti, Gian-Carlo	Amahl and the Night Visitors
Pinkham, Daniel	Christmas Cantata
Poulenc, Francis	Gloria
	Organ Concerto
Rachmaninoff, Sergei	Solemn Vespers
Ravel, Maurice	Pavanne
Rimsky-Korsakov	Russian Easter Overture
	March of the Nobles*
Rutter, John	Gloria
	many carols, hymns, and anthems
Sibelius, Jean	Finlandia
Tchaikovsky, Peter	Cappriccio Italiene
	1812 Overture
	Romeo and Juliet
Vaughan Williams, Ralph	Hodie
Verdi, Guiseppe	Requiem*
Vierne, Louis	"Kyrie"
Walton, William	Belshazzar's Feast
Willcocks, Sir David	carols and hymns

A collection of African-American spirituals

presented but not premiered

To order additional copies of:

The Splendor of His Music

send $12.99 plus $3.95 shipping and handling to:

Books, Etc.
PO Box 1406
Mukilteo, WA 98275

or have your credit card ready and call:

(800) 917-BOOK

To receive more information about Music Mission Kiev and the continuing story of the McMurrins through the newsletter "The Gazetta" please write to the following address:

Music Mission Kiev
P.O. Box 56-0578
Orlando, Florida 32856

Questions about the ministry may be addressed through e-mail at the following addresses:

MMKiev@aol.com
or
diane@mmk.kiev.ua